COLOUR TEST PAGE

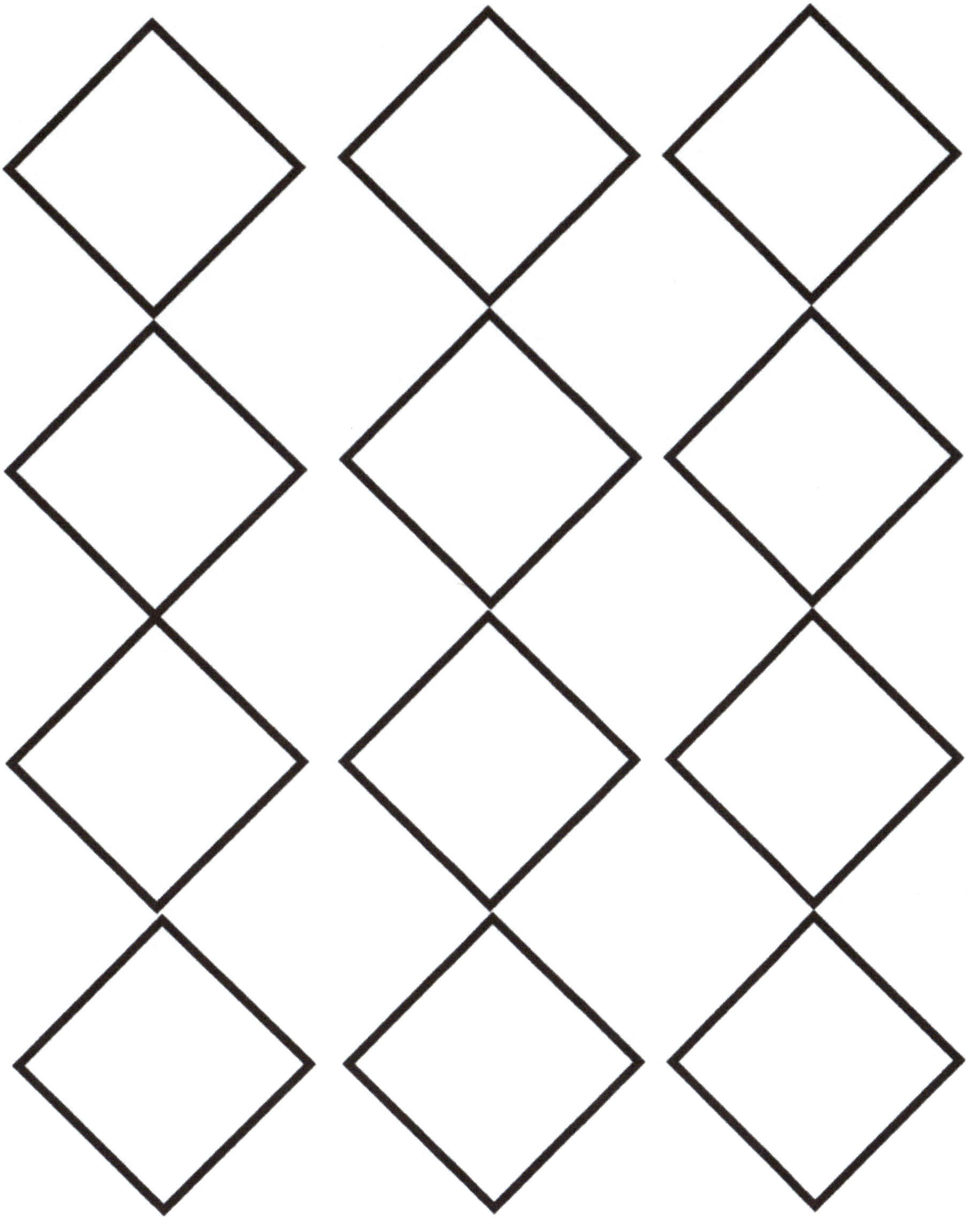

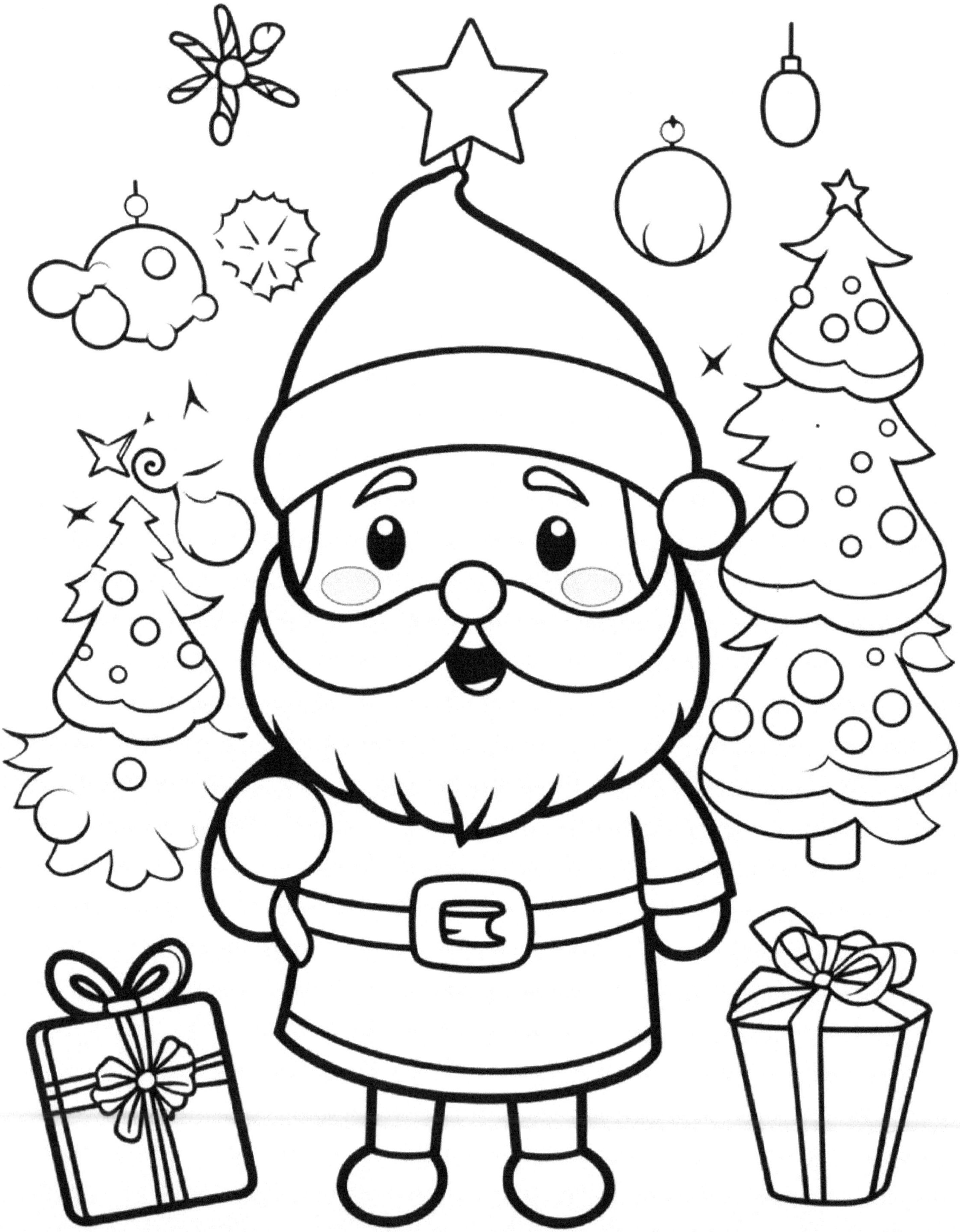

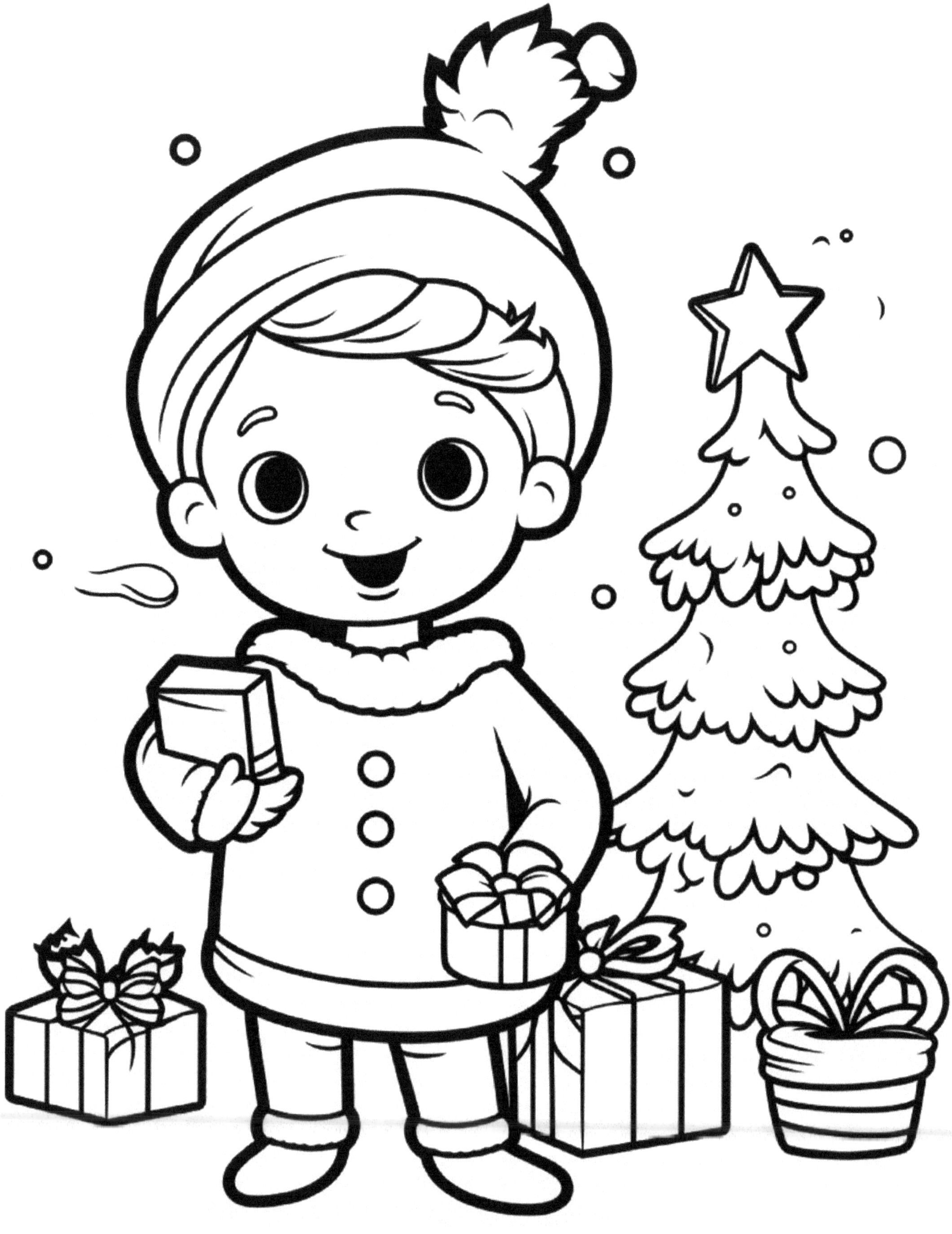

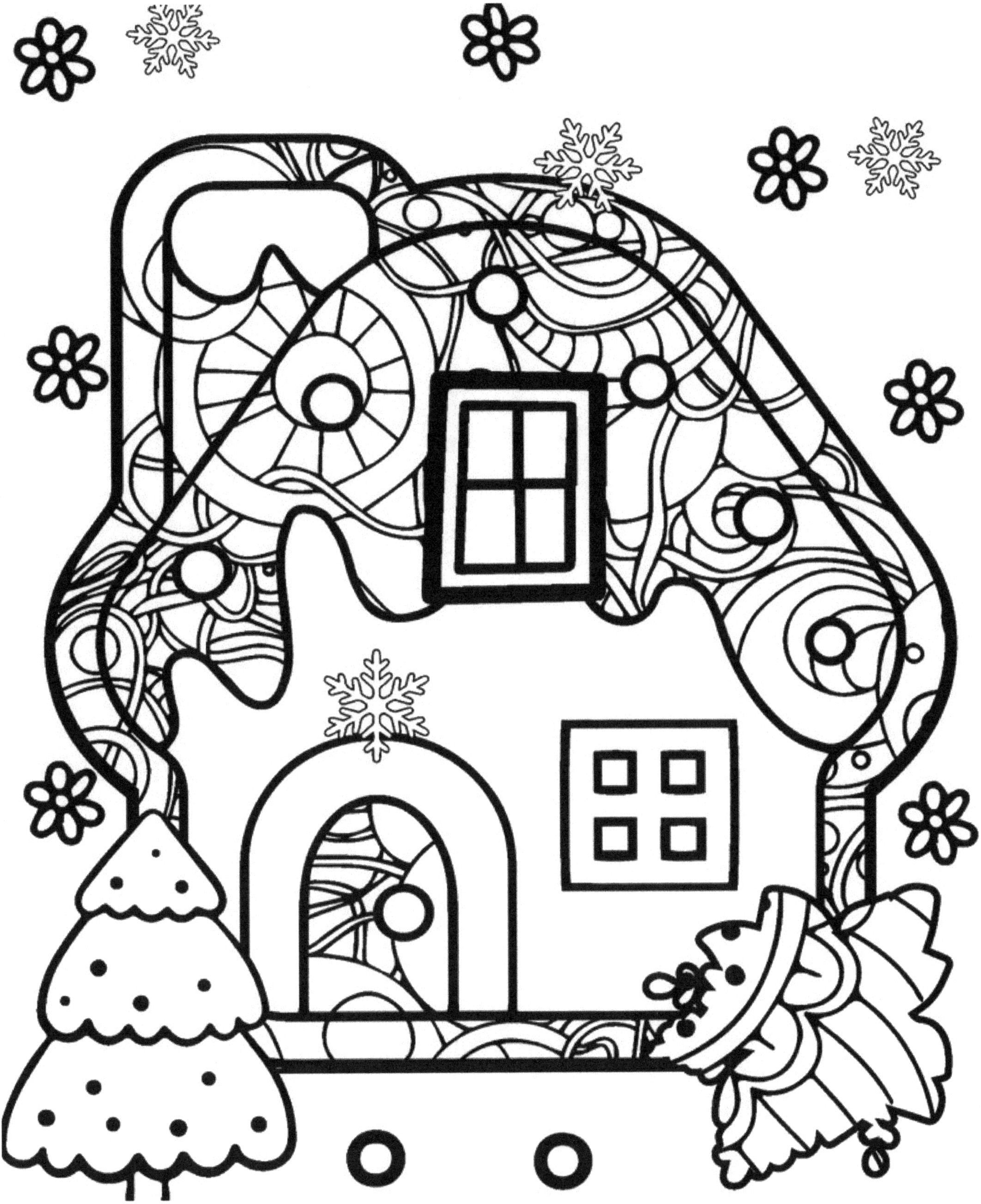

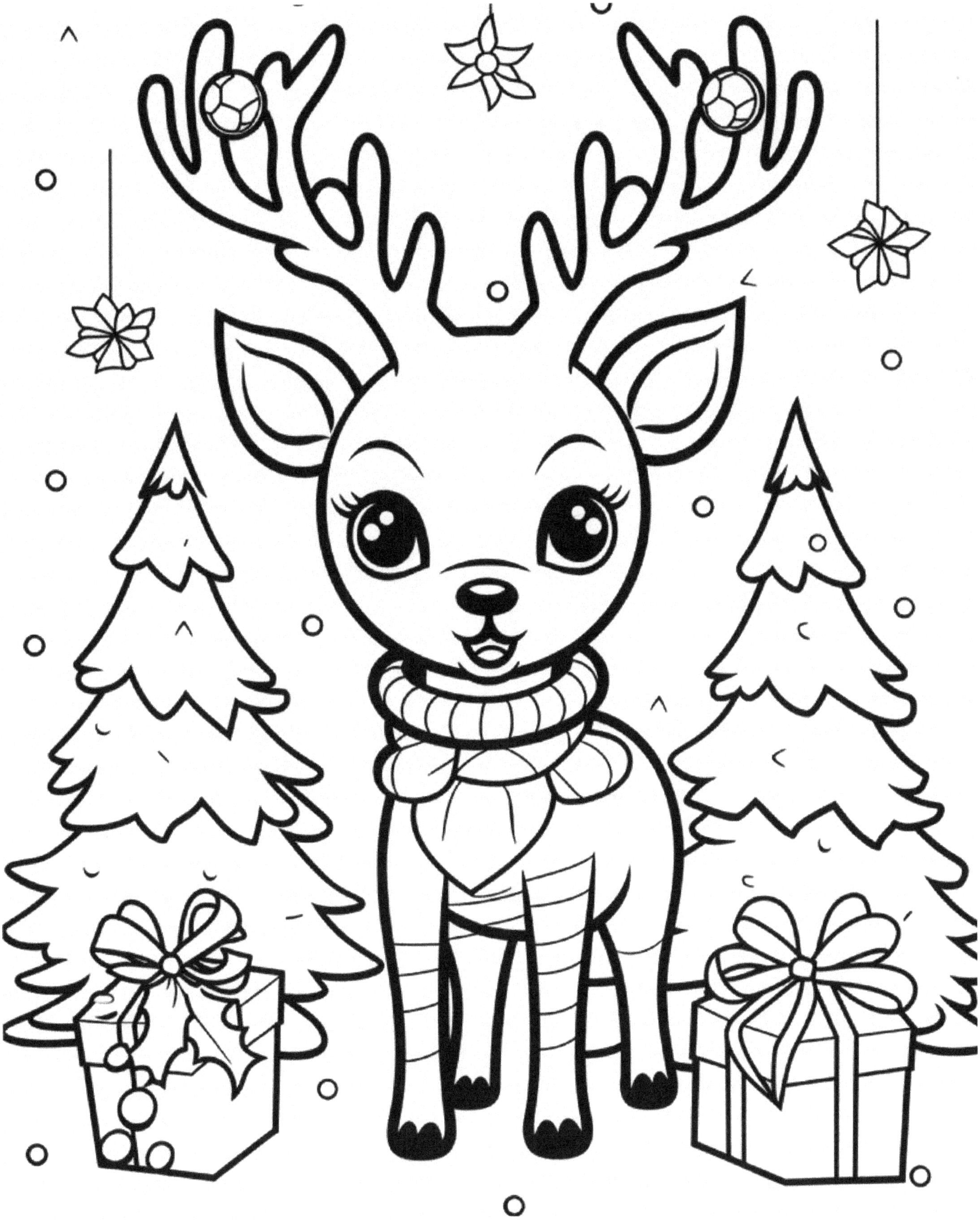

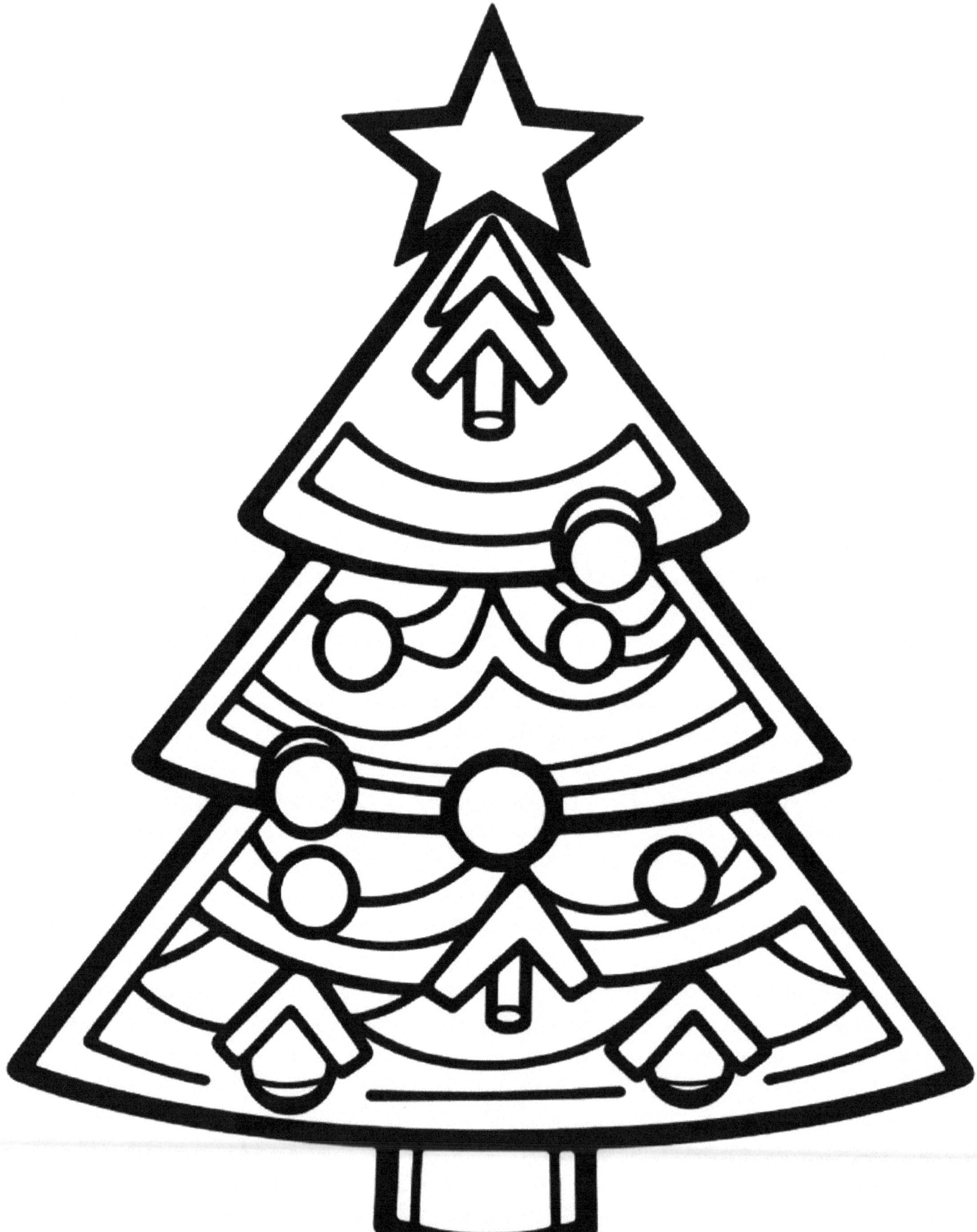

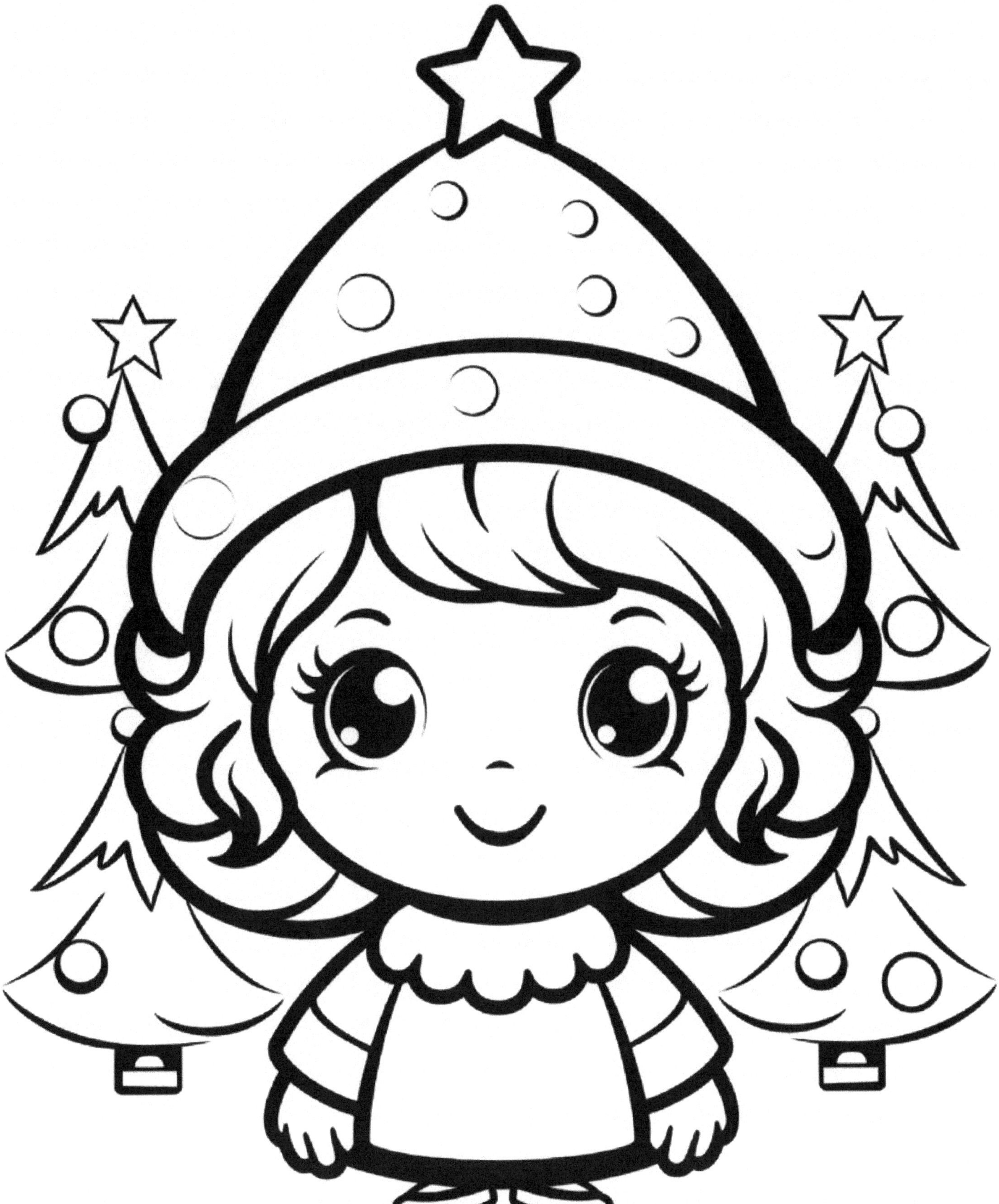

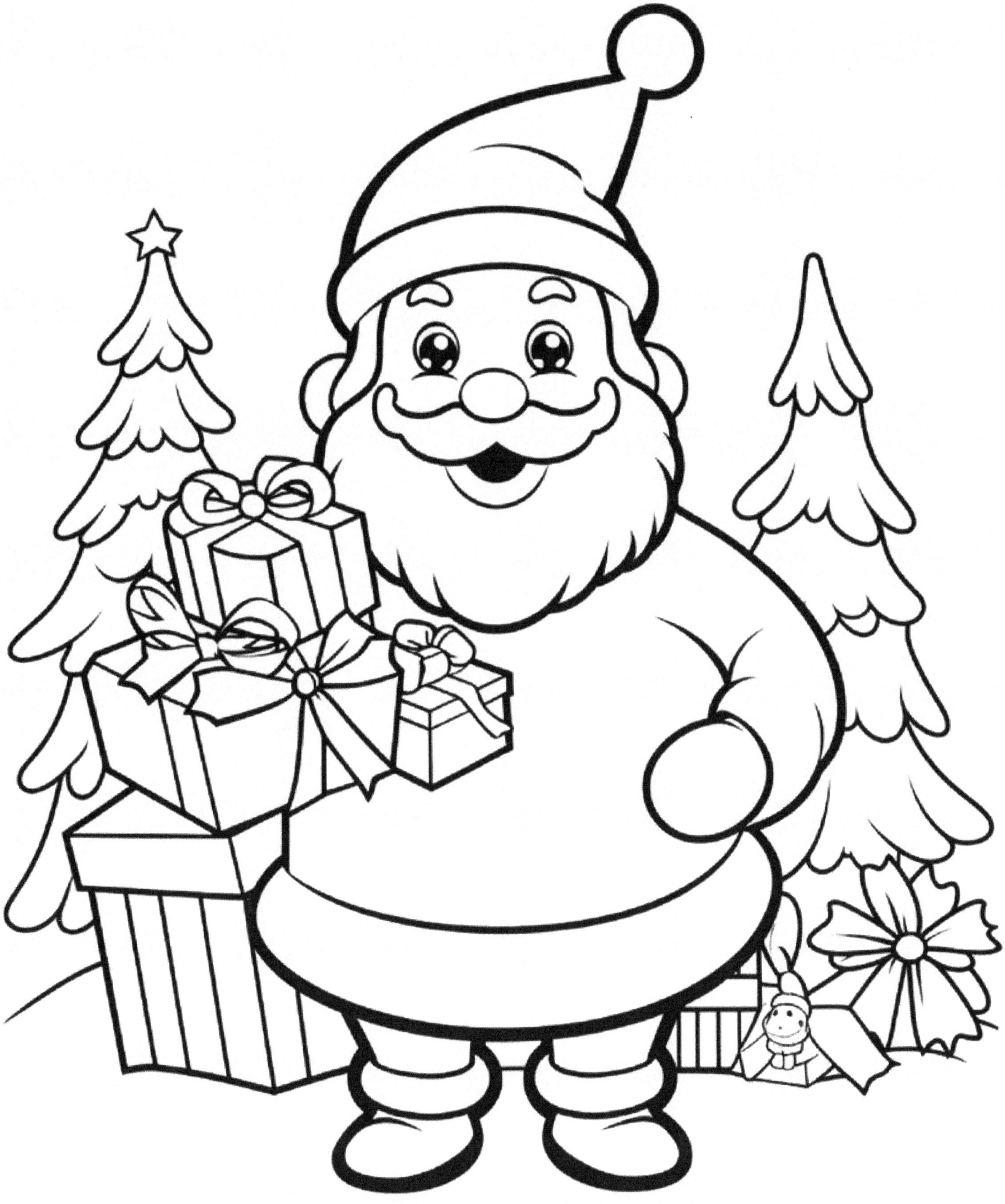

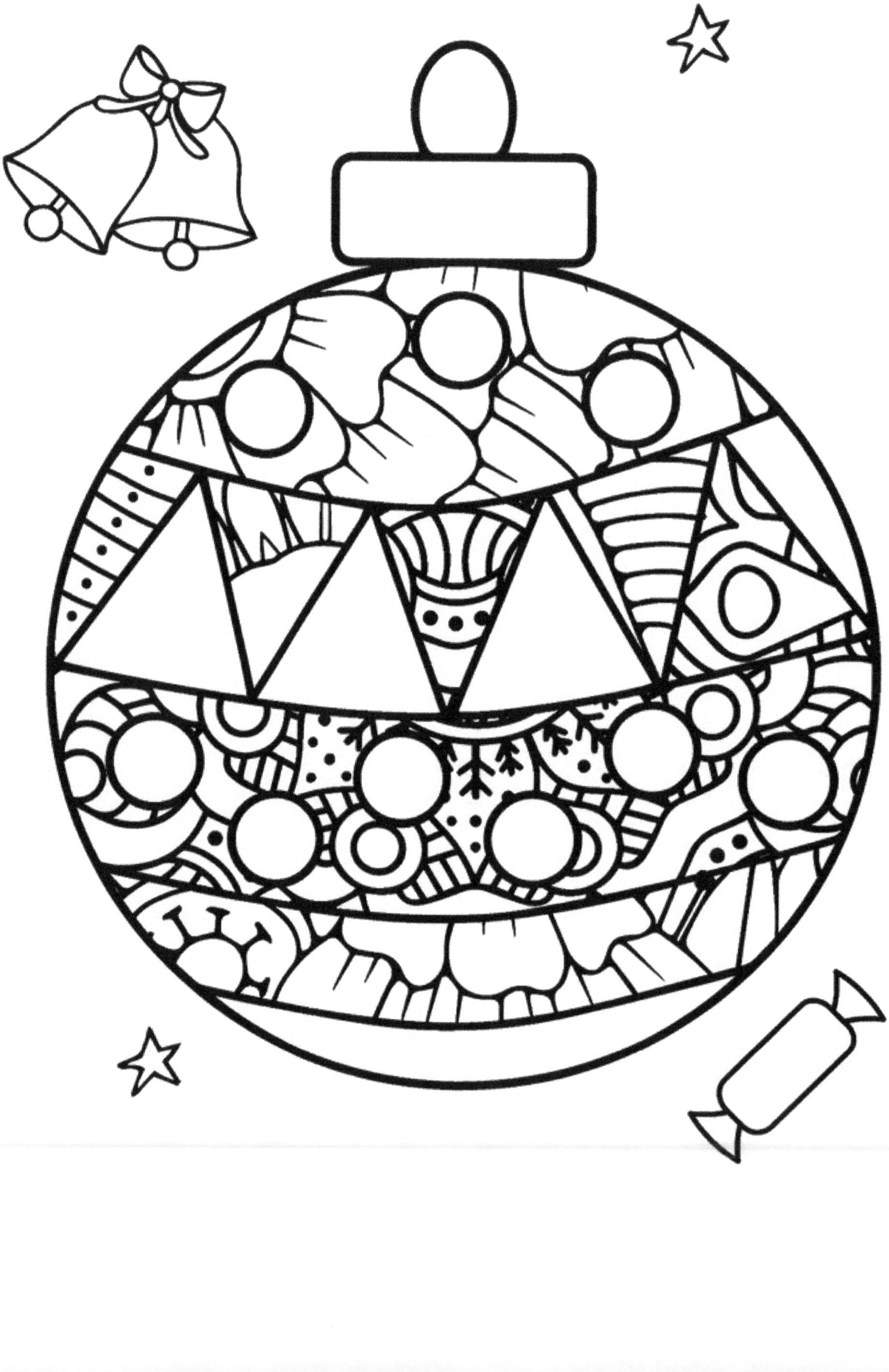

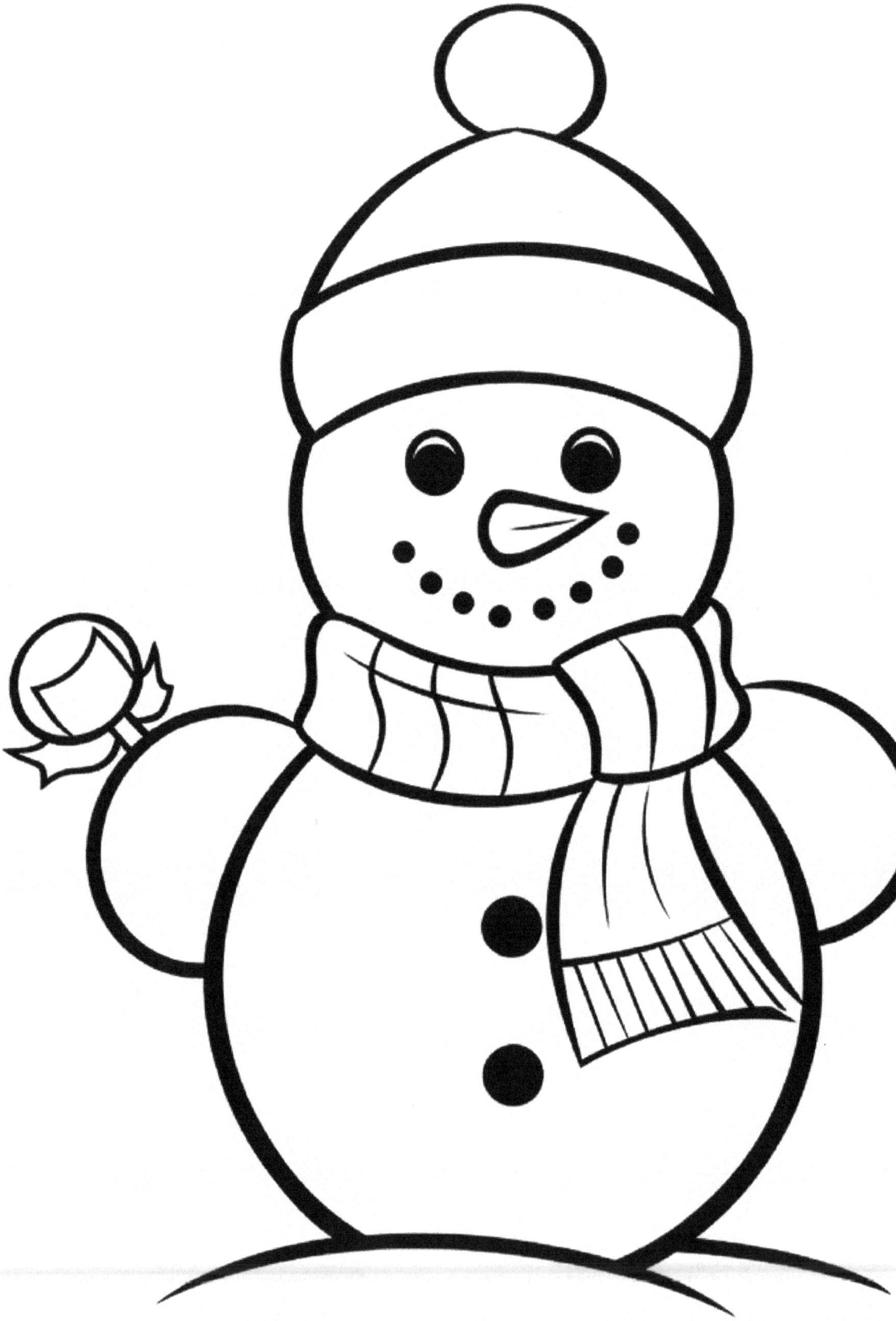

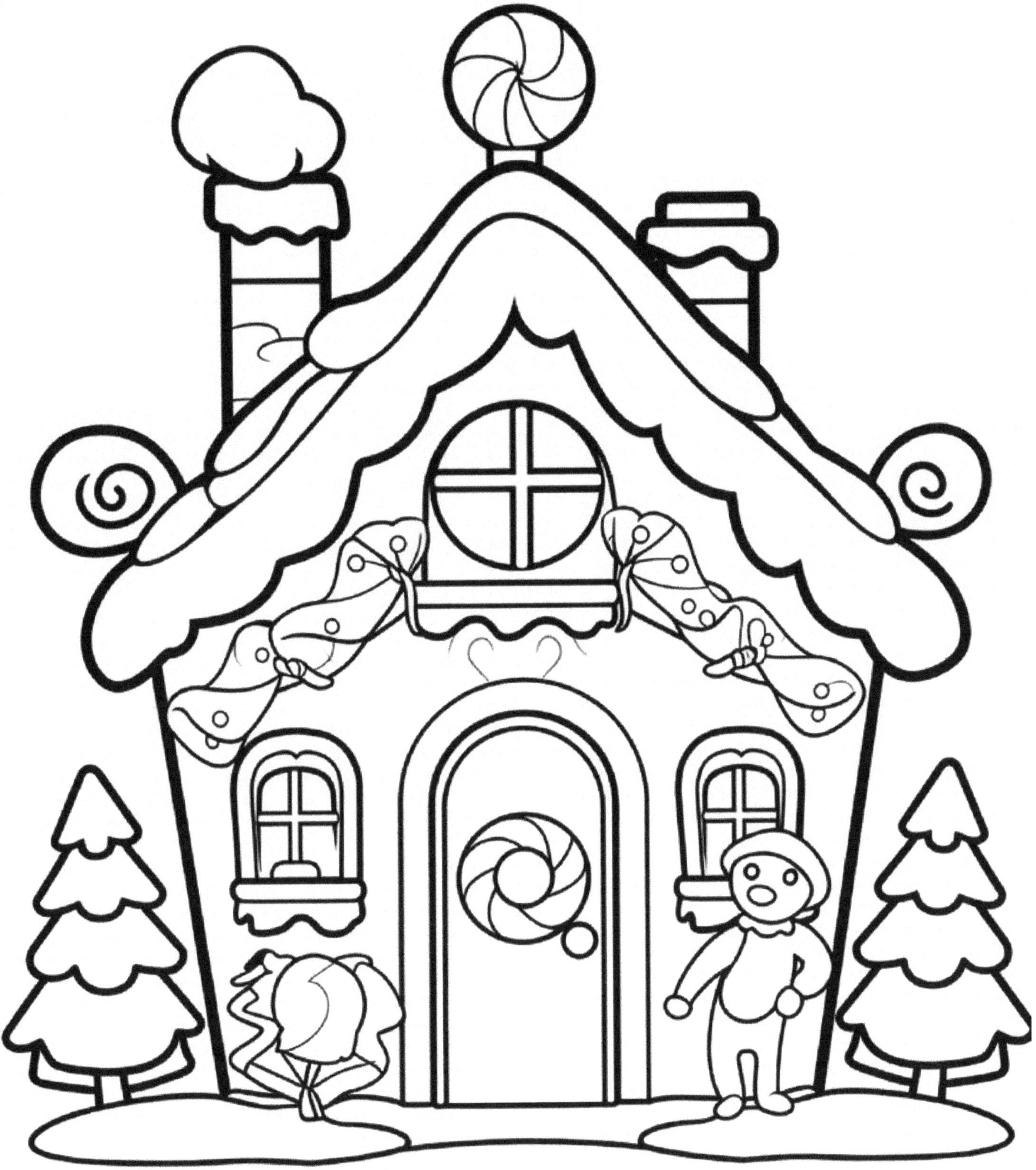

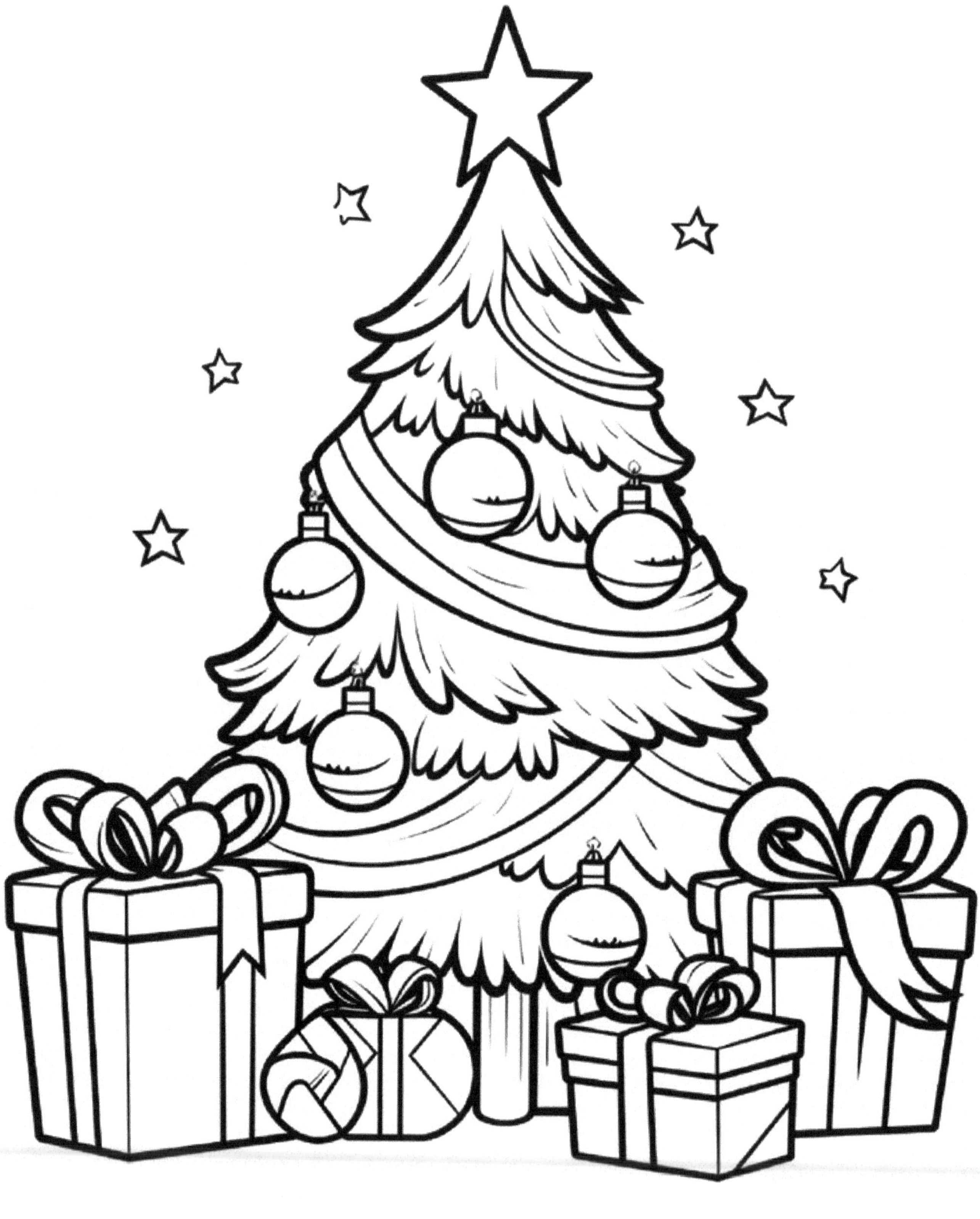

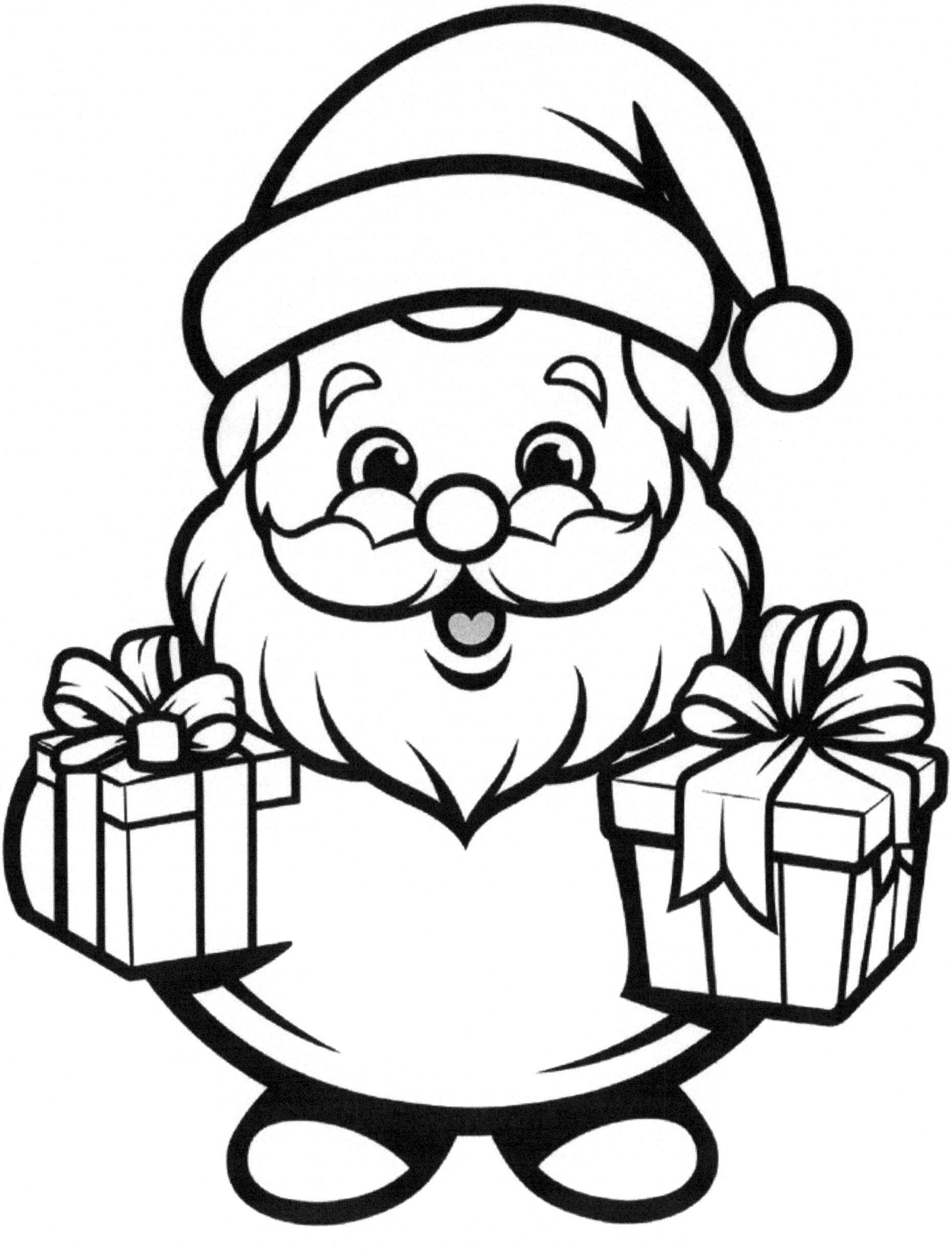

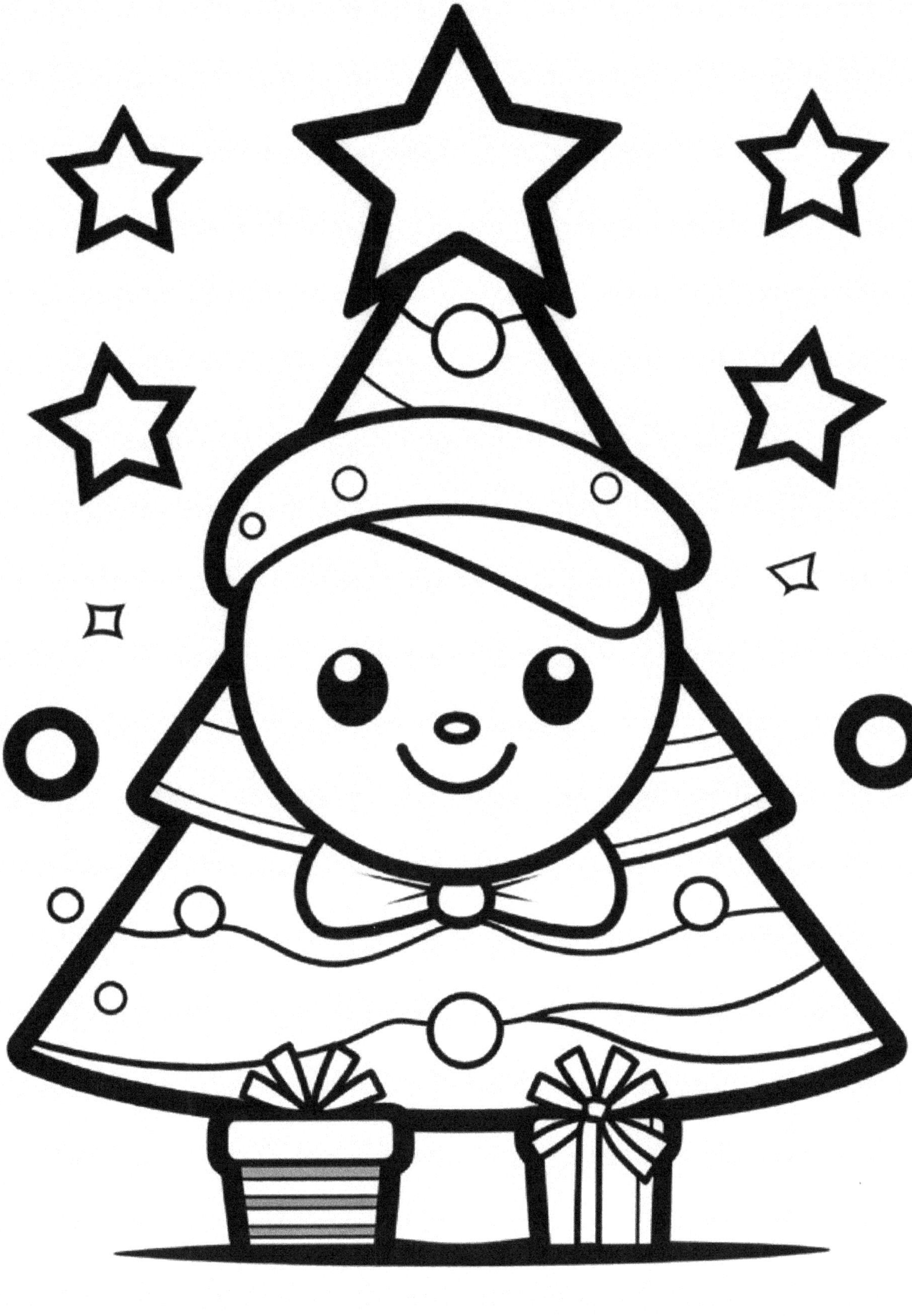

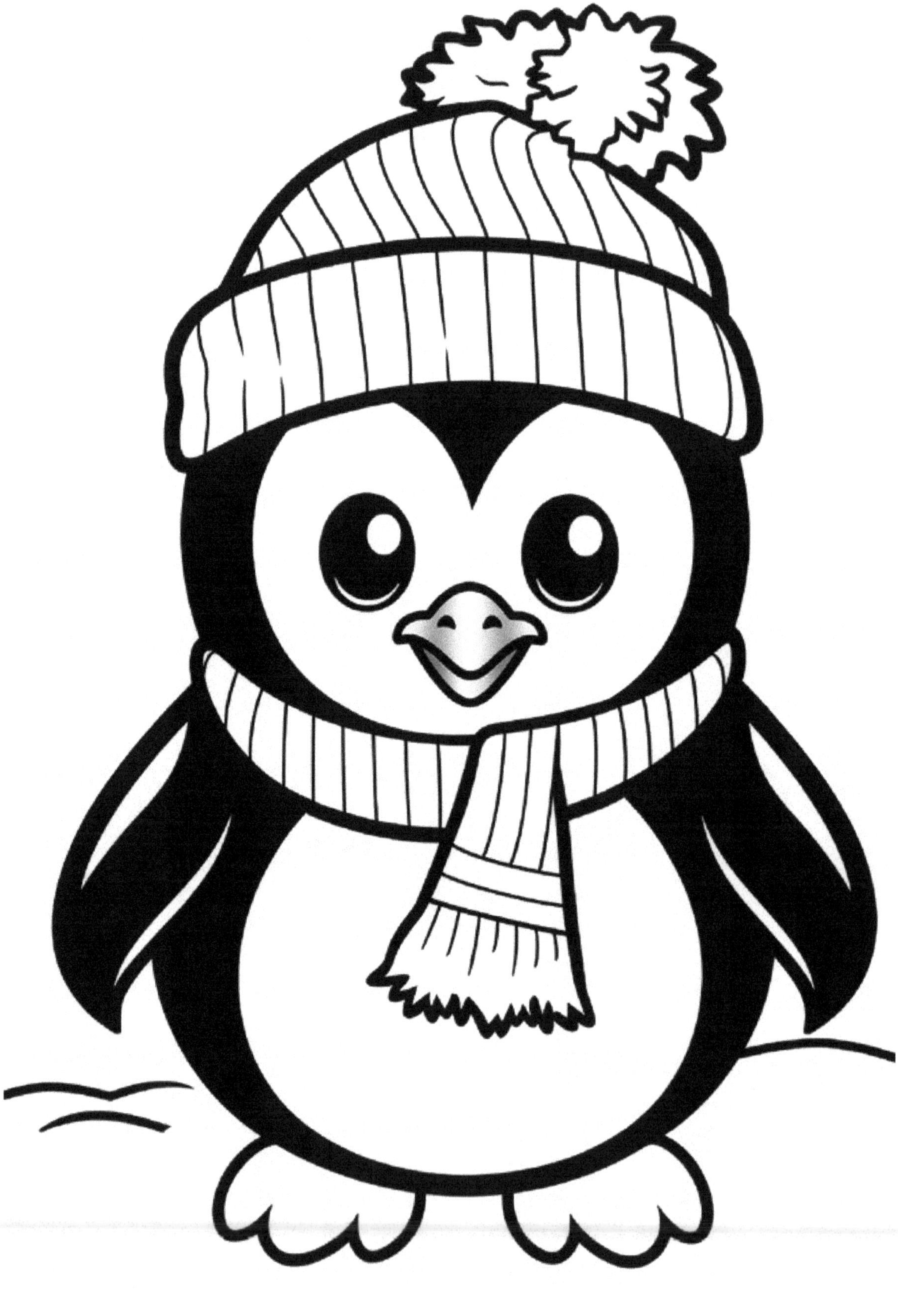

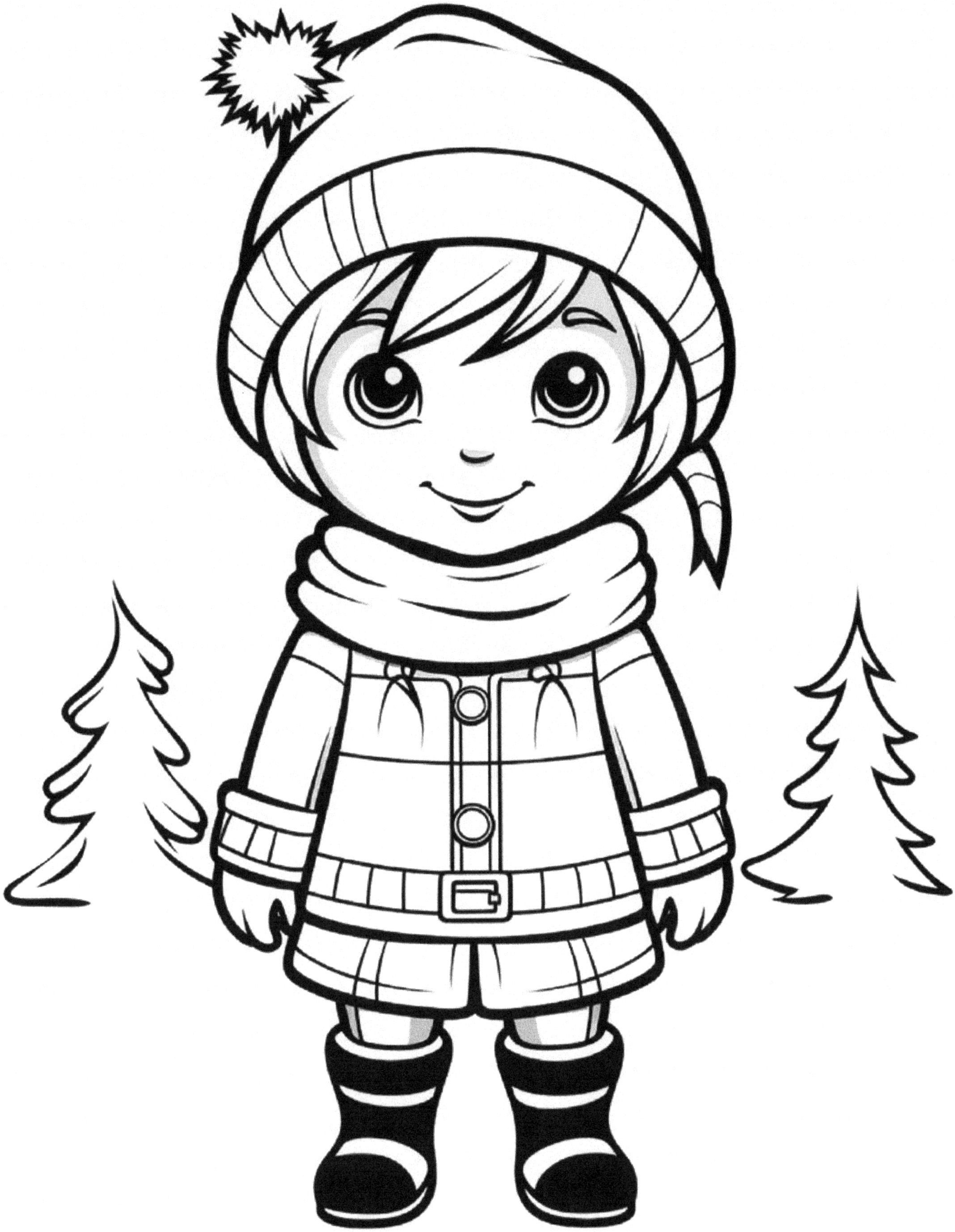

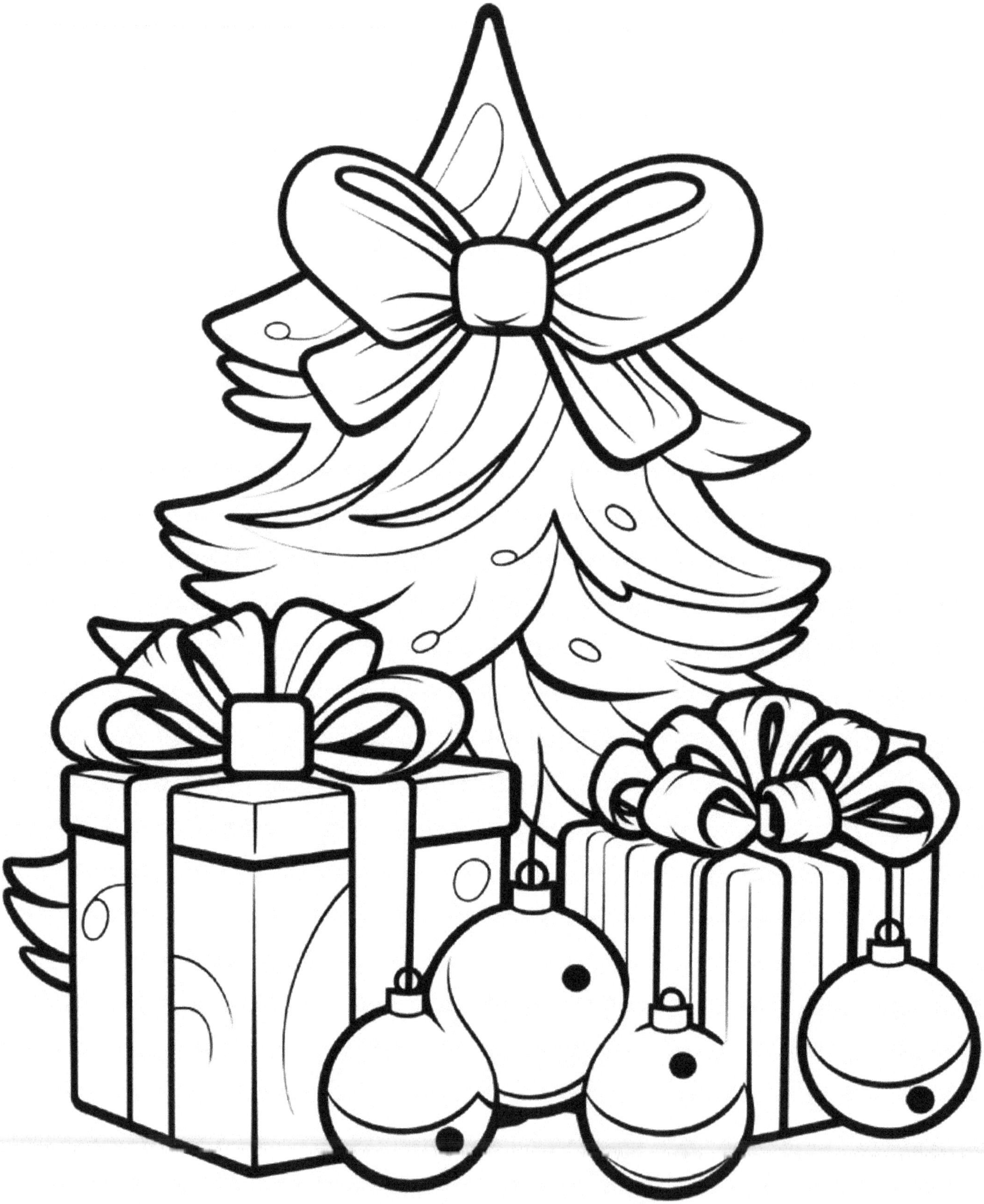

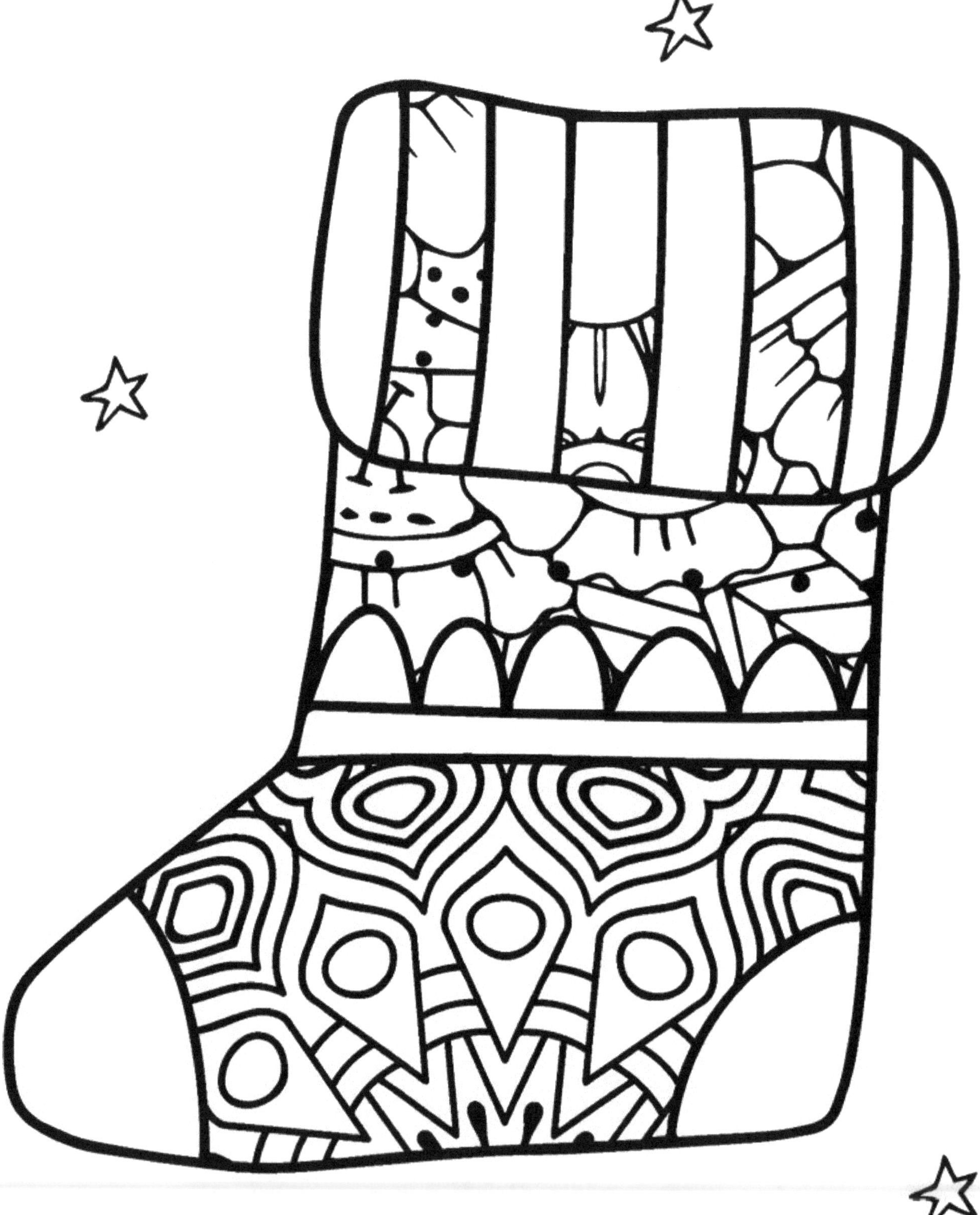

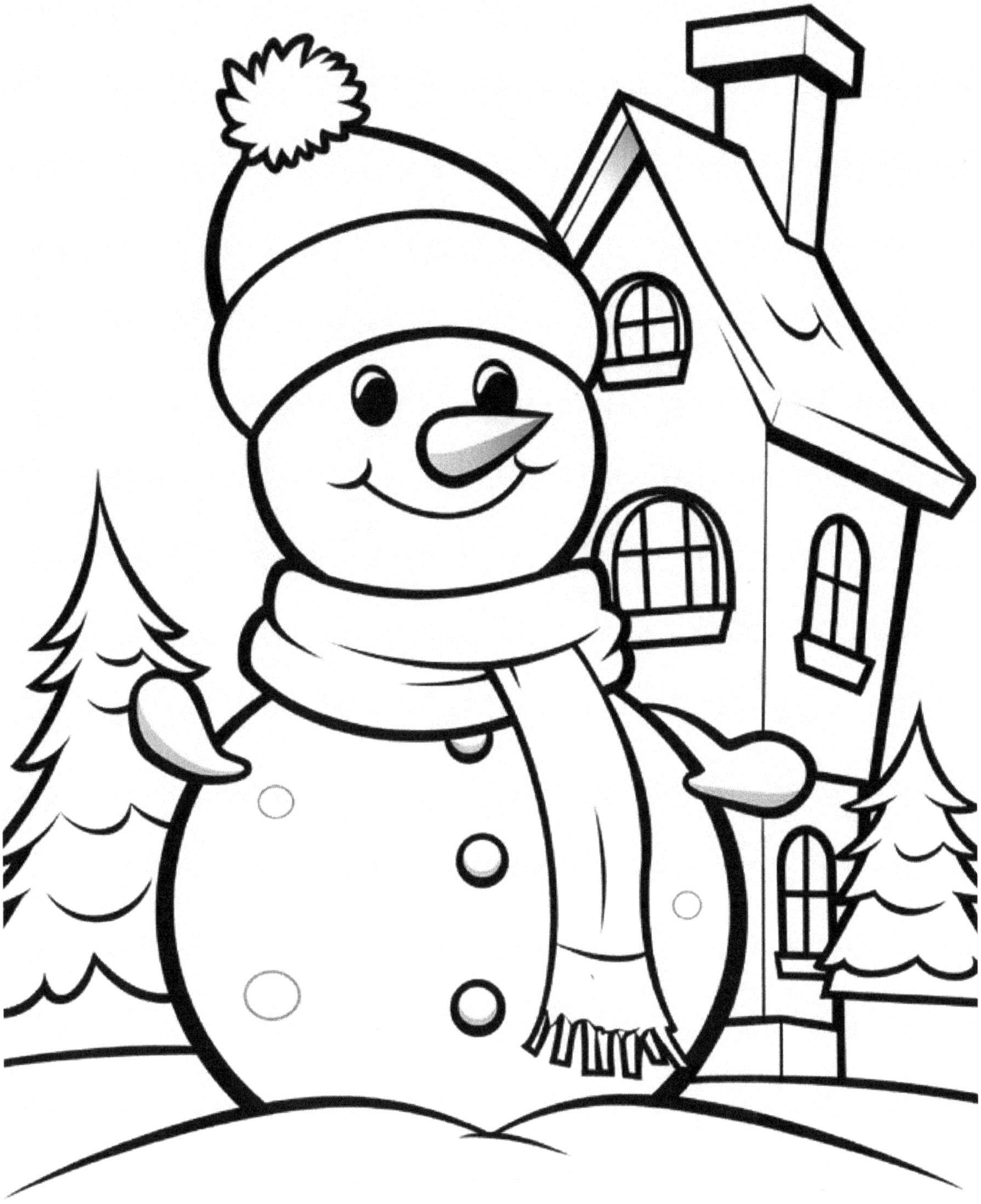

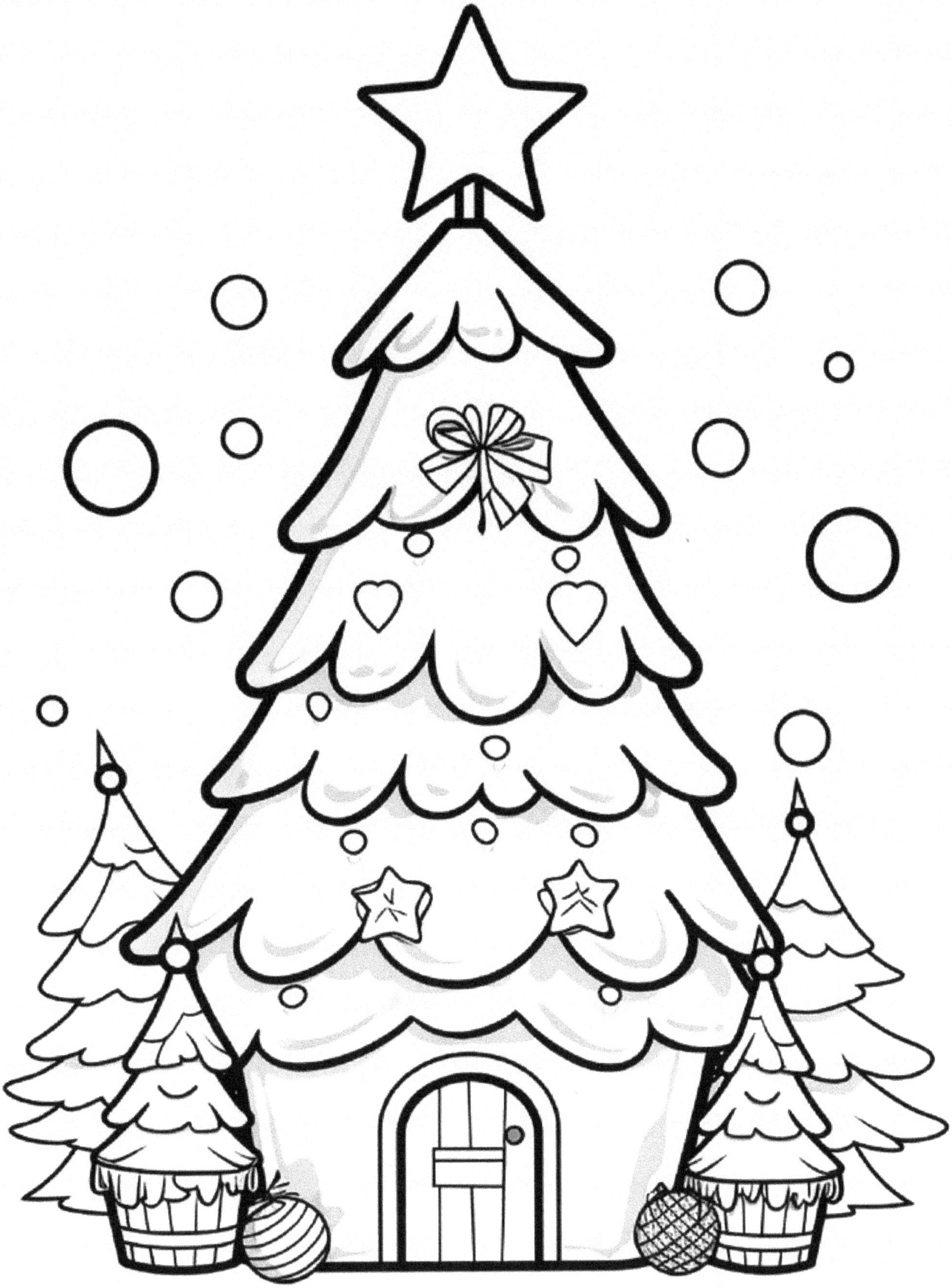

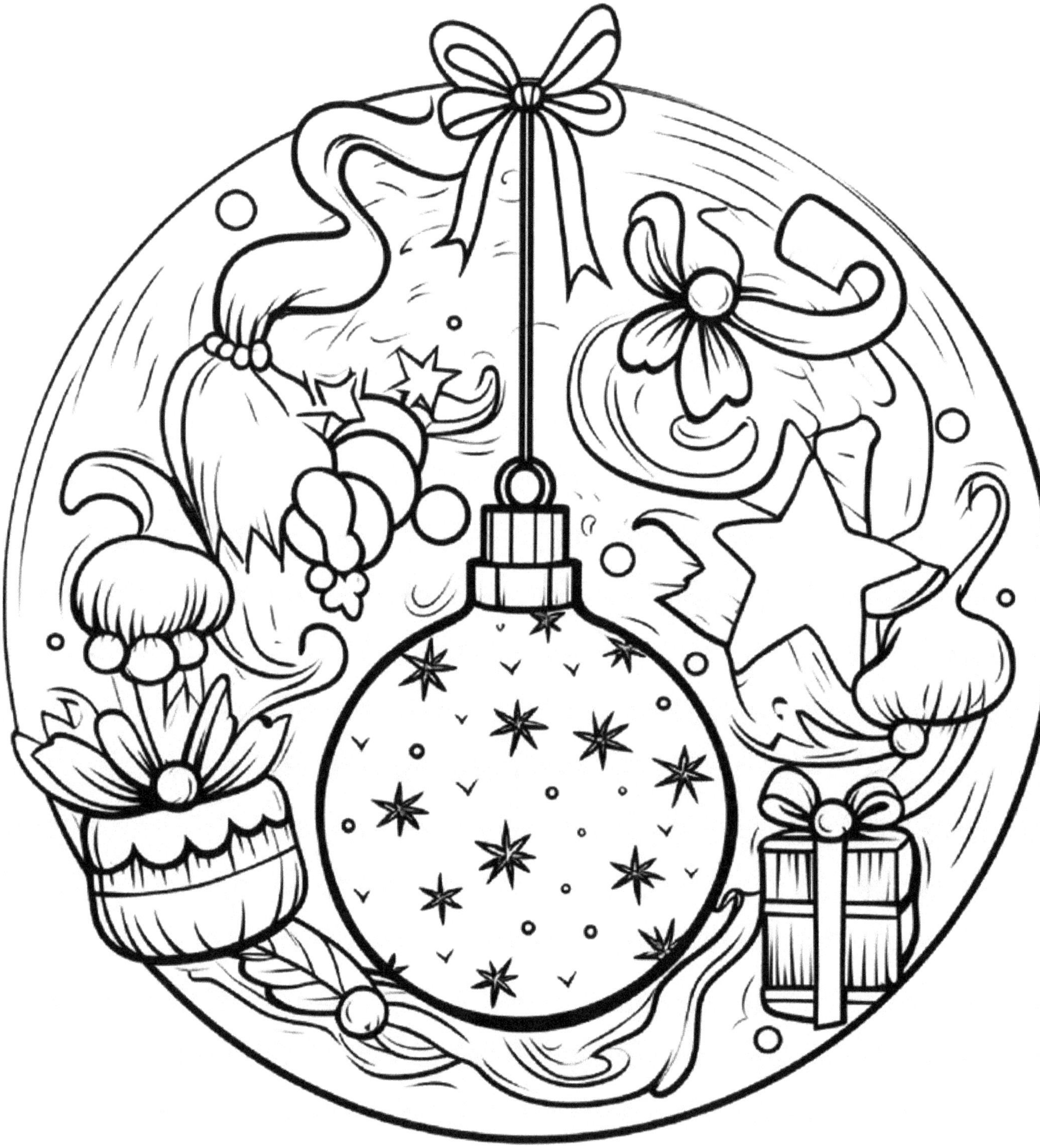

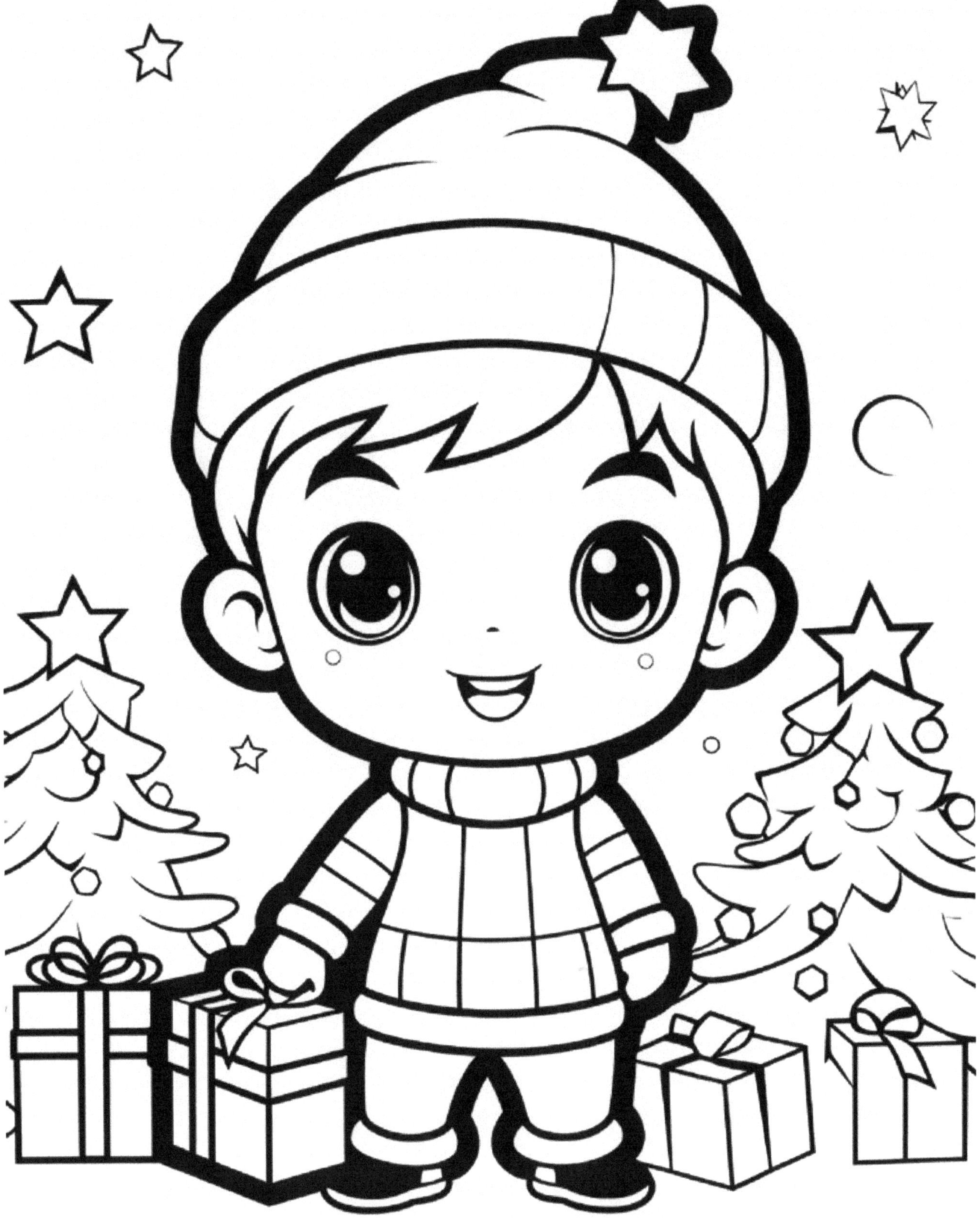

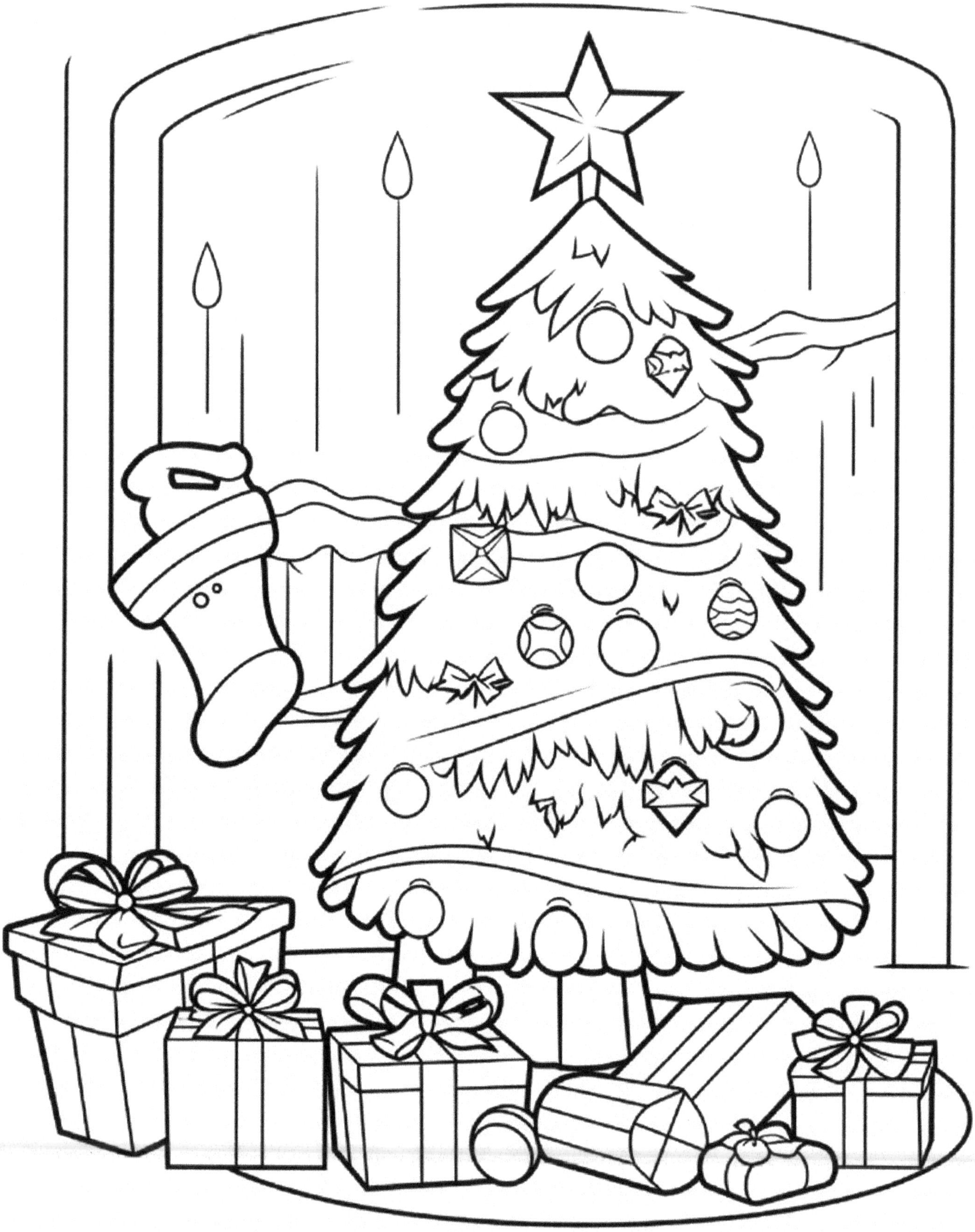

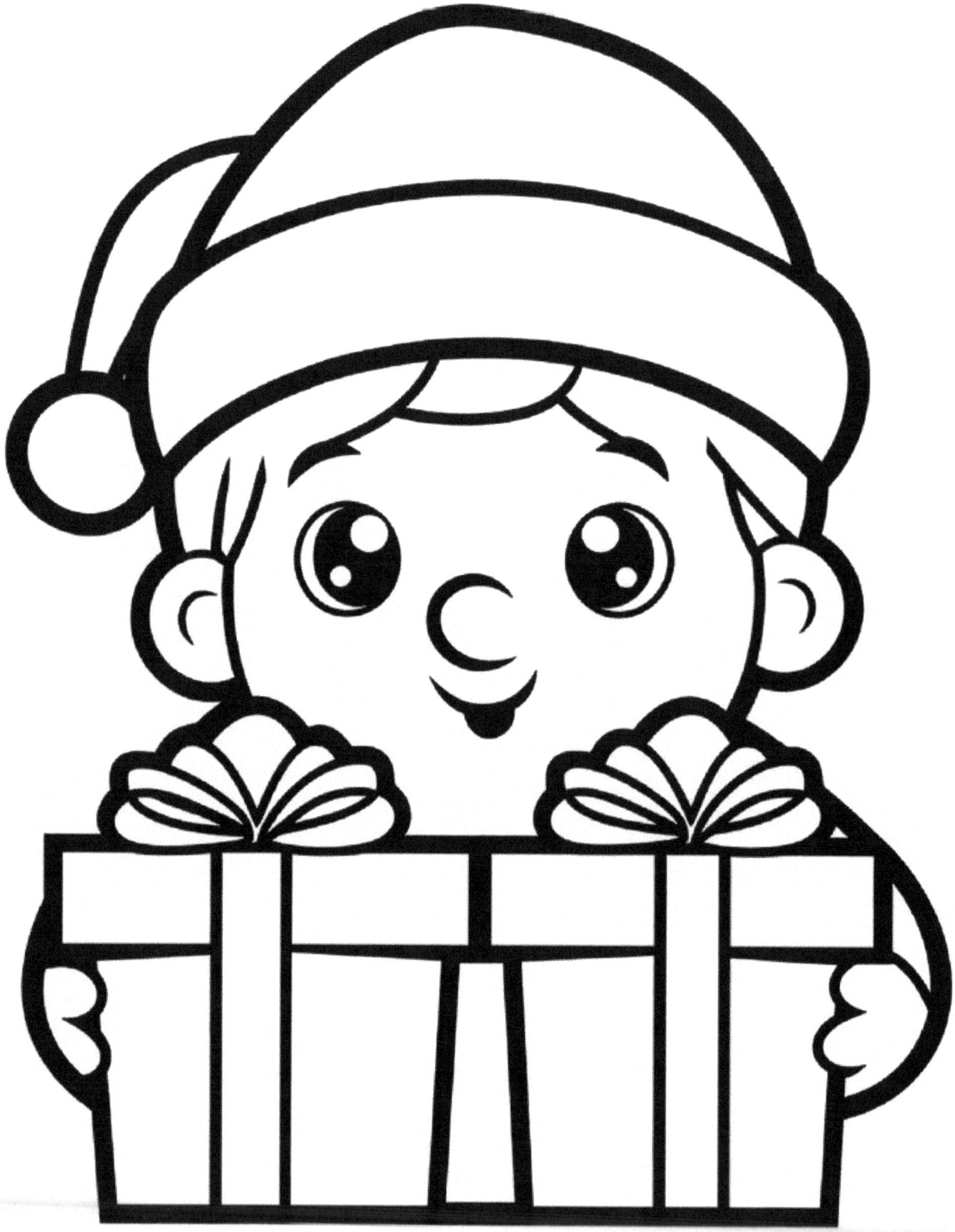

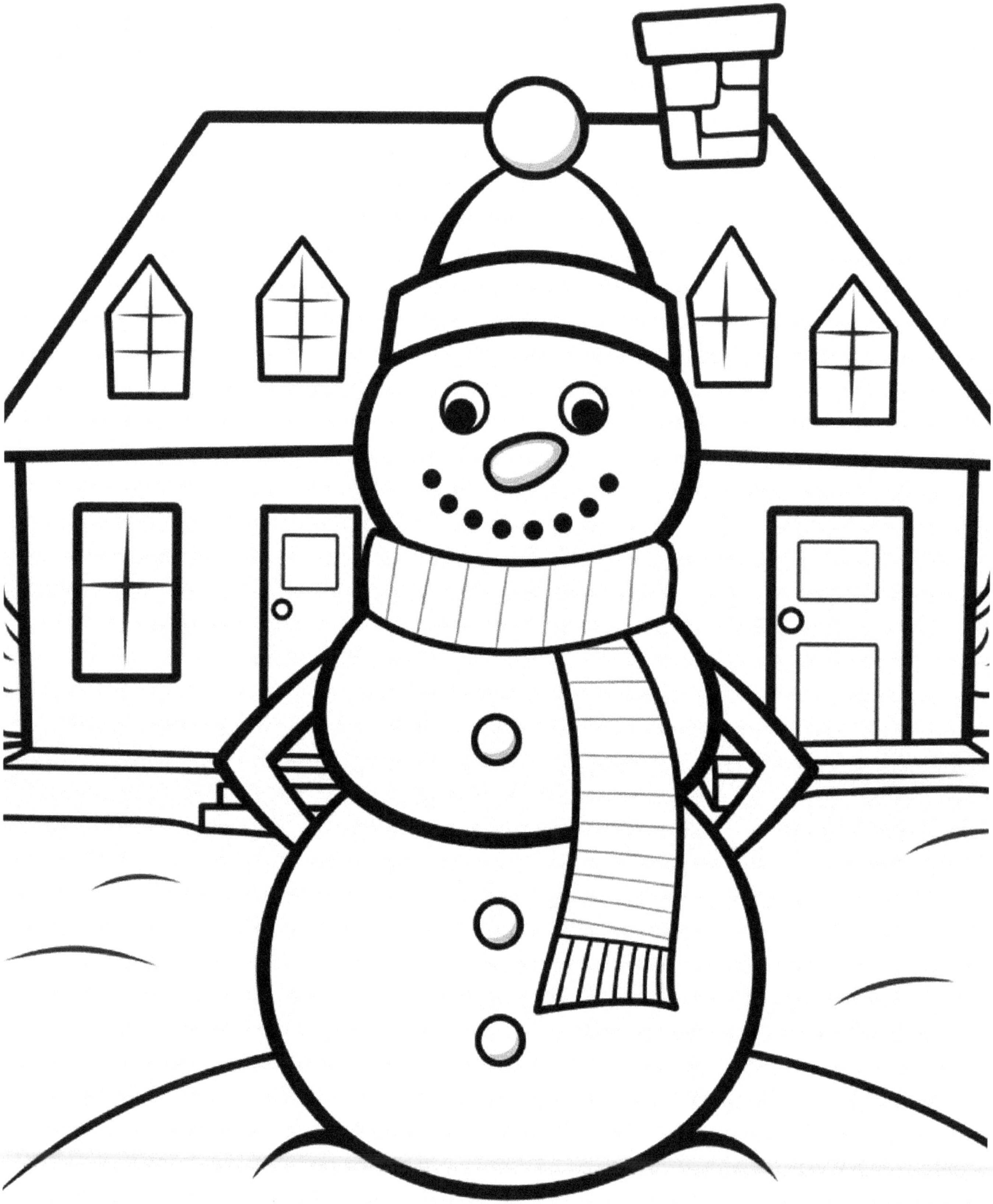

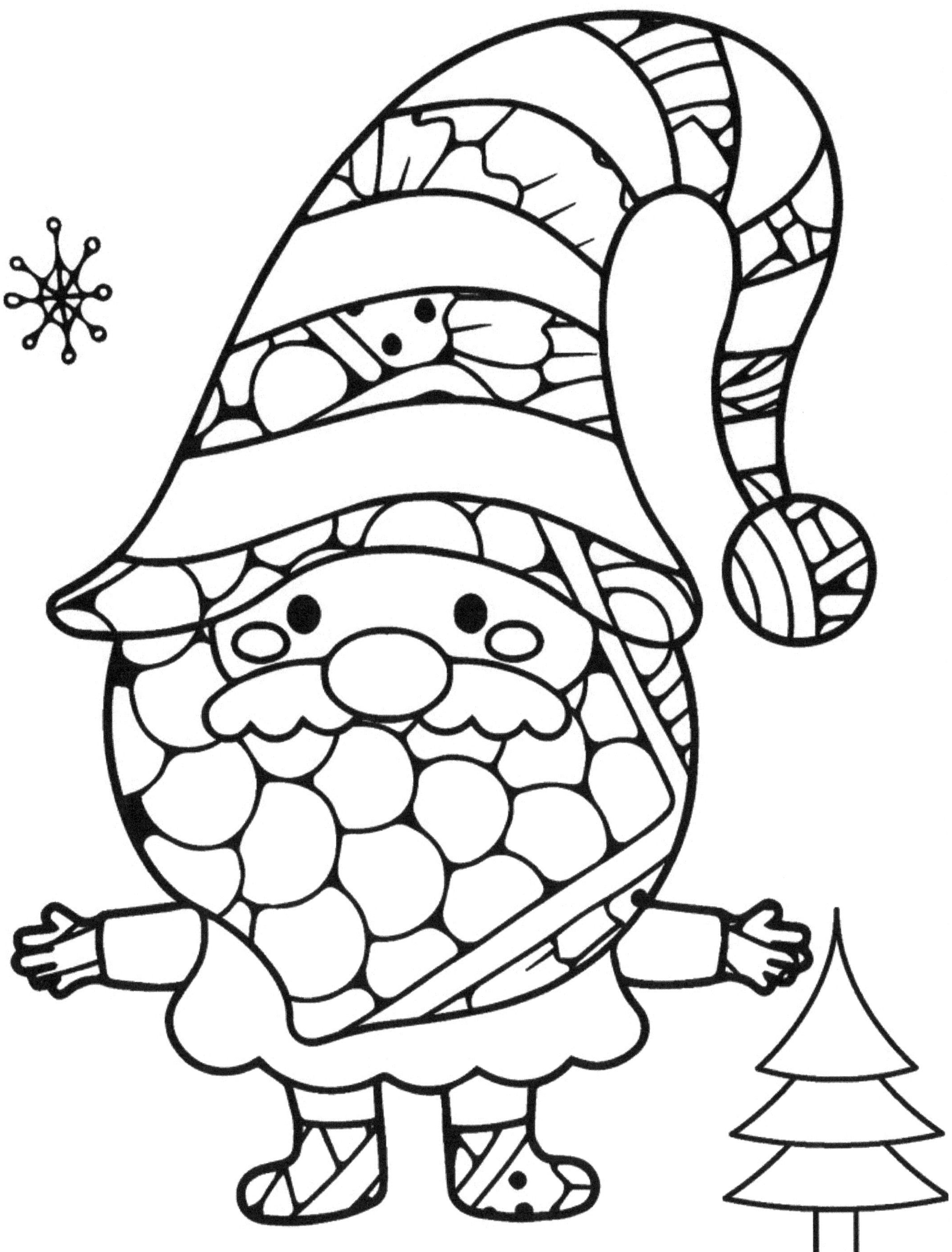

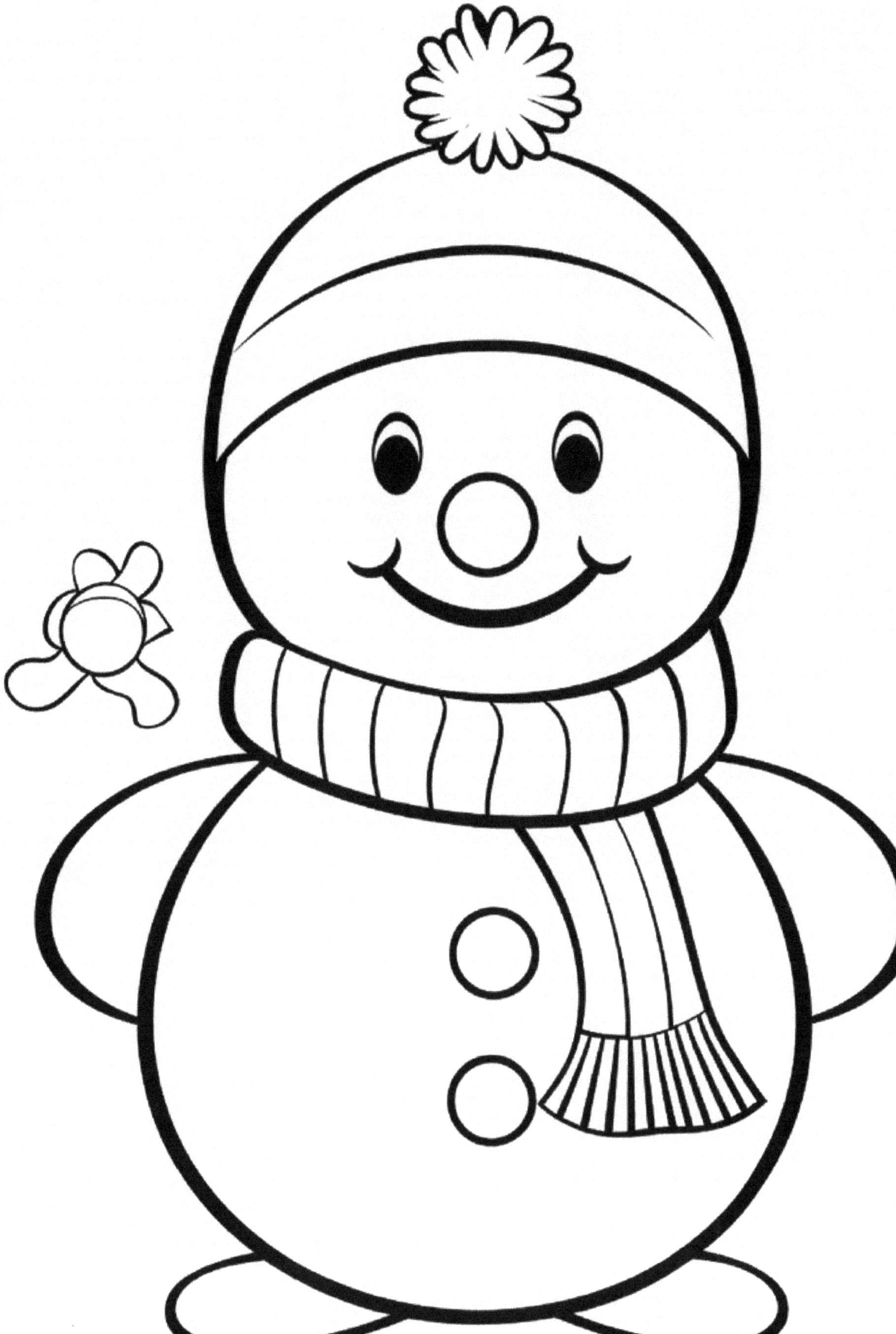

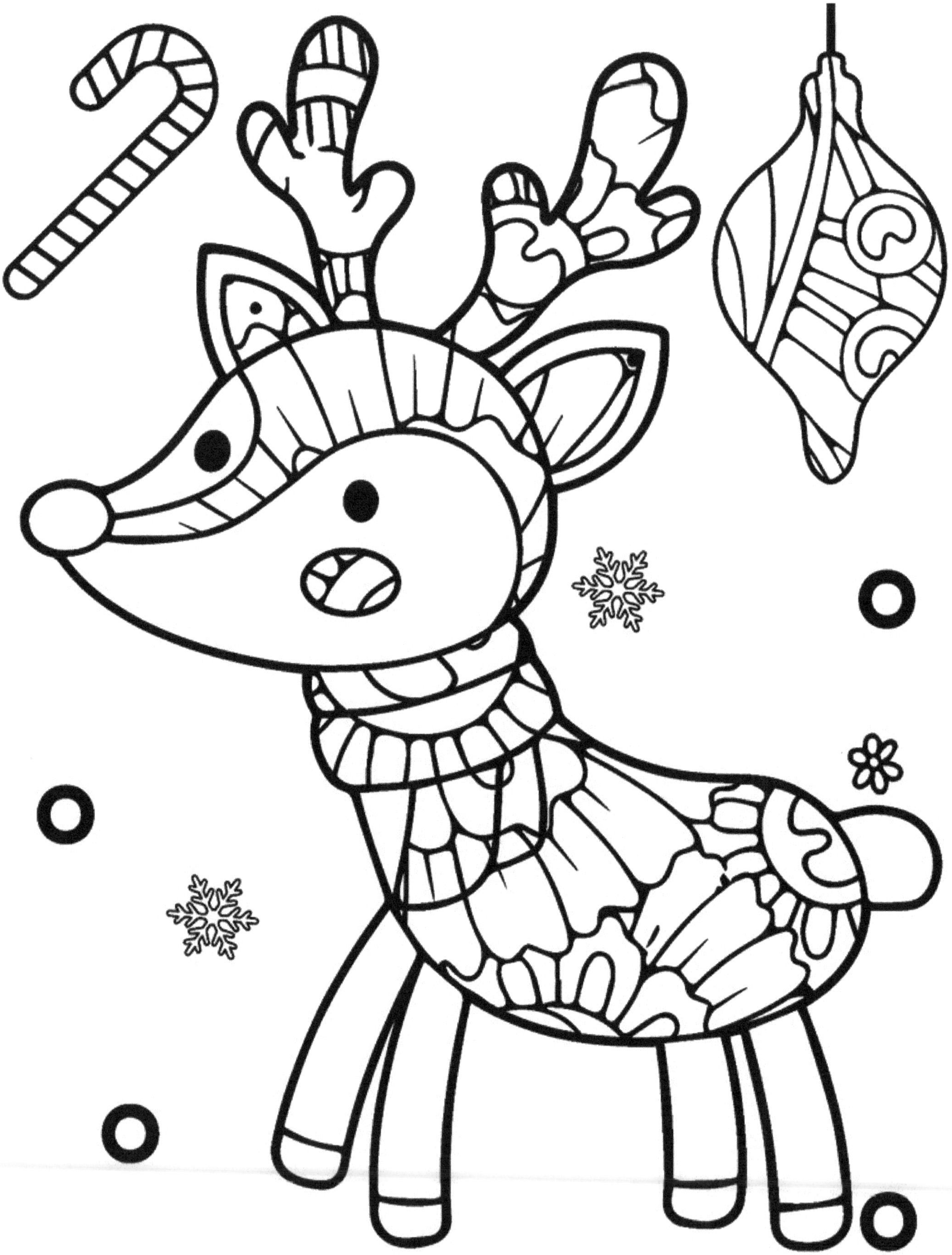

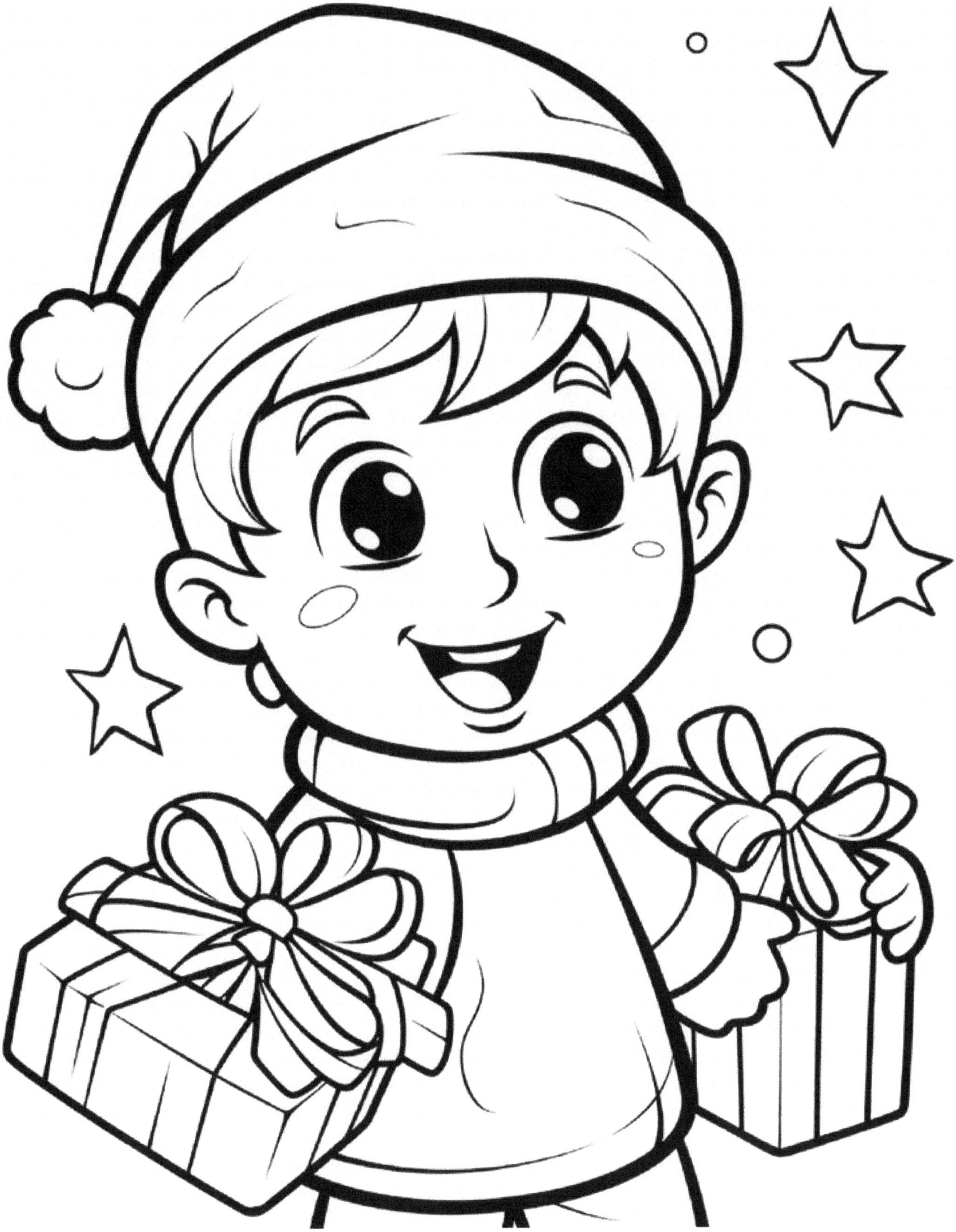

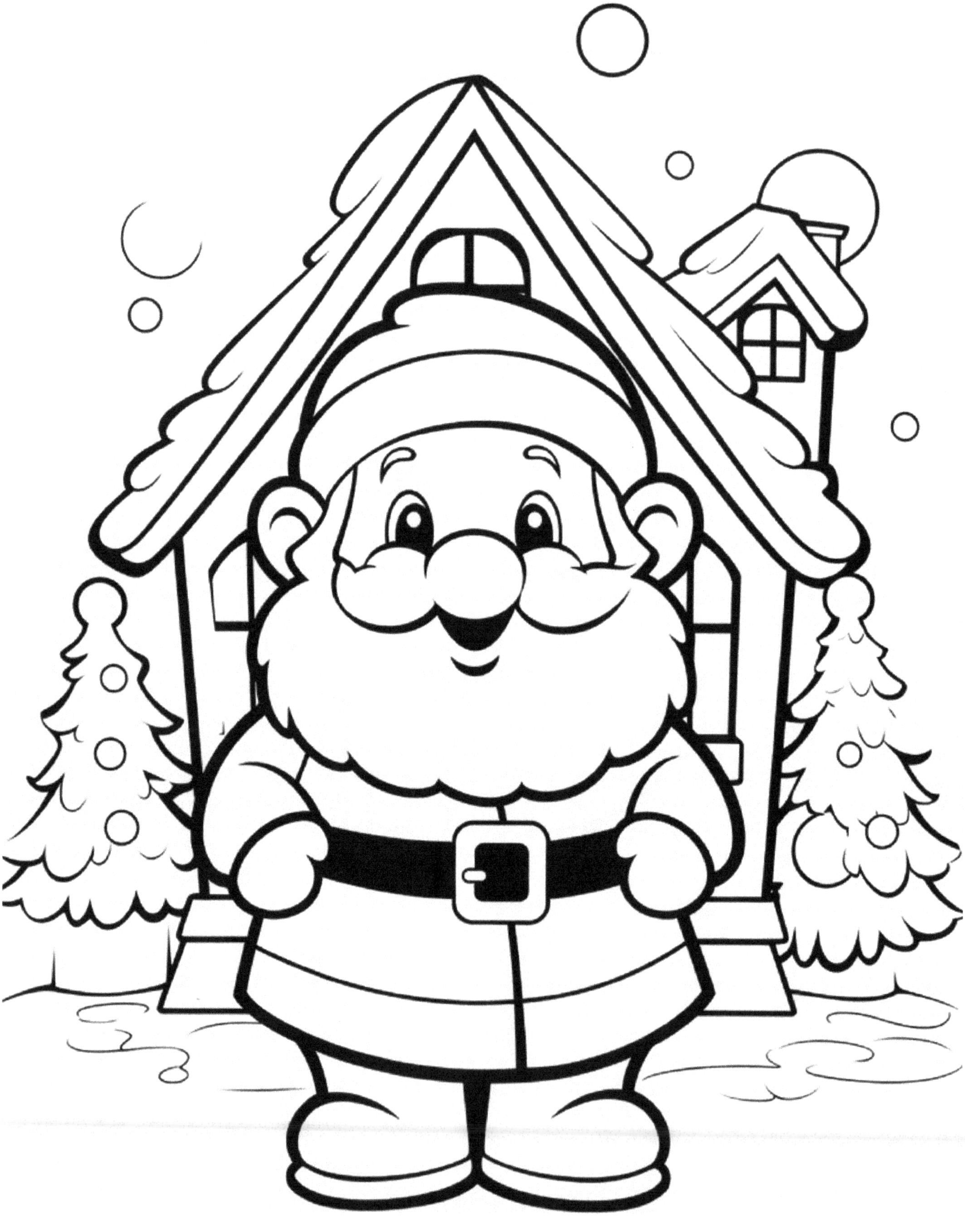

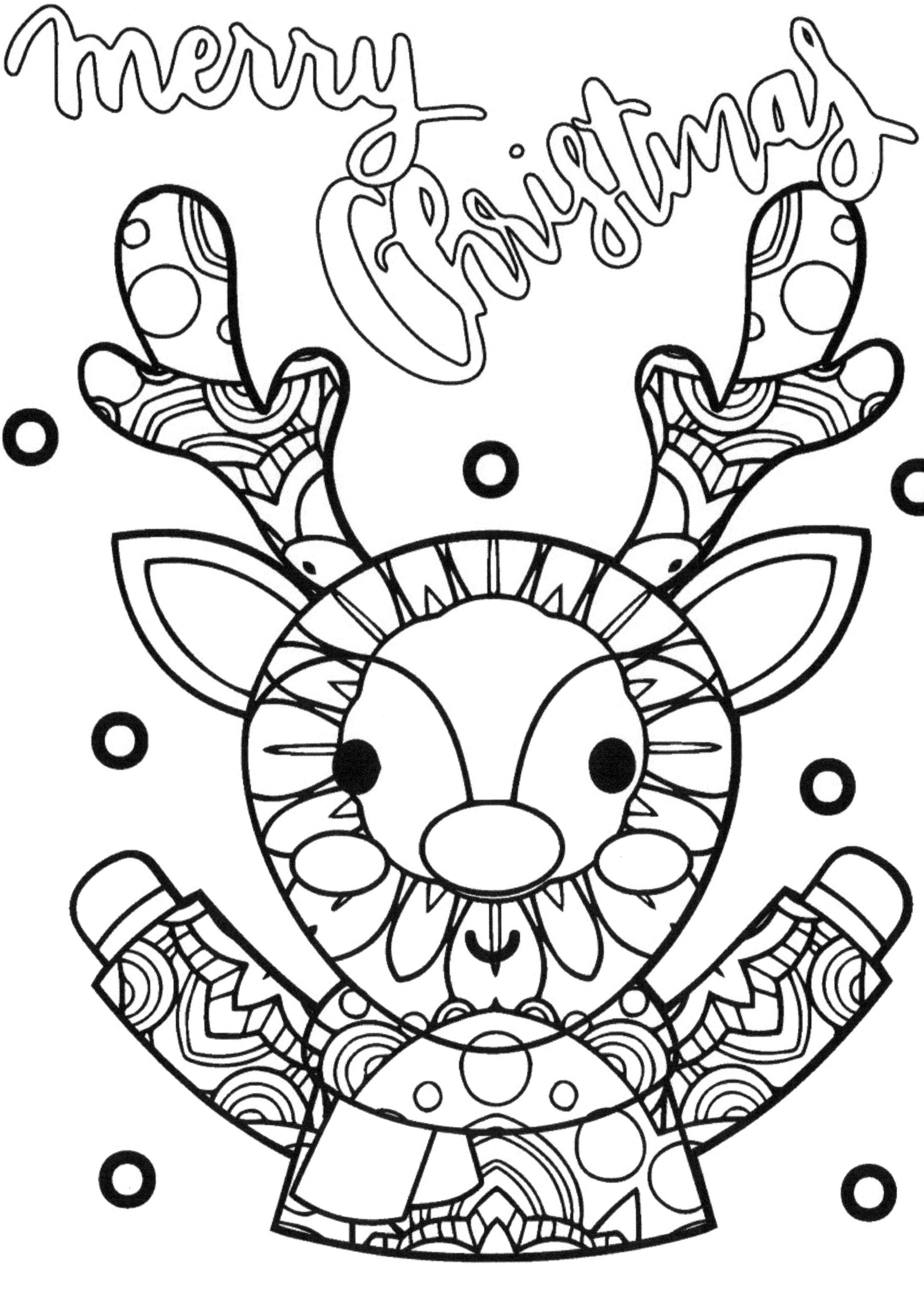
Merry Christmas

THANK YOU

www.ingramcontent.com/pod-product-compliance
Lightning Source LLC
Chambersburg PA
CBHW041128120626
46547CB00019B/2899
9798889408840